Are You Really Free?

Reflections On Christian Freedom

Richard Stoll Armstrong

Fairway Press, Lima, Ohio

ARE YOU REALLY FREE?

FIRST EDITION
Copyright © 2002
Richard Stoll Armstrong

ISBN 0-7880-2032-3   PRINTED IN U.S.A.

Dedicated
with a grandfather's
affection and pride
to
Derek, Gray, Ryan,
Alyssa, Olivia,
and Seth

Foreword

Freedom is never free. It requires constant vigil and sacrifice and sometimes the sacrifice of human life. Christians understand that better than anyone, because for them the sacrifice of Christ's life on the cross is the ultimate expression of God's desire that we be free from an insecure life without him.

But as Richard Armstrong points out so well in this book, human beings often place their security in things that seem to promise freedom but that ultimately fall short. "There is no ultimate security in the things which human beings and nations are predisposed to turn to for security," writes Armstrong. "Our security is in God" (pp. 215, 216).

Are You Really Free? is a book for those who think. It is about more than just freedom. It is for those who grapple with faith issues. It is not just another devotional book. It is written by one who brings considerable insight and skill to the question of how we can be truly free and what constitutes real freedom, the kind Christ intends for all people. The author tackles the difficult issue of belief in God and moves it from merely an acknowledgment of God to an investigation of a personal knowledge of God.

Armstrong's insights are laced with honest questions and thoughtful responses. He anticipates the skeptic, embraces the skeptic's doubt, and then illuminates a clear path to travel out of the darkness of doubt. I found chapter 18 to be especially helpful. It may speak to many postmodern people, even postmodern Christians, who say they do not believe in propositional truth. Everything is experience for them.

With the terrorists attacks of September 11, 2001, our nation entered into a new era. Before that infamous day we Americans had been confident that somehow security was our inalienable right. Now we know that our nation is as vulnerable to terrorism as any other nation. I suspect that those who read this book will get a wake-up call in the final chapter that now more than ever proves our faith must be in God through Christ, and not in our American way of life. I view that as a powerful conclusion to this book.

For those who wish to know God and experience liberating freedom in an insecure world, *Are You Really Free?* is an essential contribution.

Ronald W. Johnson
Professor of Mission and Evangelism
McAfee School of Theology, Mercer University

What's It All About?

"For freedom Christ has set us free; stand firm, therefore, and do not submit again to a yoke of slavery.... For you were called to freedom, brothers and sisters ... " (Galatians 5:1,13a). These two affirmations by the apostle Paul are truly two of the most liberating texts in the entire Bible, but not in the way some liberation theologians have used them. They are not a political manifesto. The "yoke of slavery" to which the apostle Paul refers is not physical bondage or servitude, but the self-imposed yoke of the Hebrew Law, which no one could fully live up to and therefore earn one's salvation by perfect obedience.

Nor is the freedom Paul talks about a guarantee of liberation from persecution and oppression. Nor is it precluded by bodily enslavement. On the contrary, freedom in Christ cannot be overcome by tyranny or stifled by subjugation. It is a kind of freedom the world cannot understand, the kind the early martyrs knew when they sang their way to death in the Roman Colosseum, the kind that enabled the apostle Paul to declare, " ... We are more than conquerors through him who loved us. For I am convinced that neither death, nor life, nor angels, nor rulers, nor things present, nor things to come, nor powers, nor height, nor depth, nor anything else in all creation, will be able to separate us from the love of God in Christ Jesus our Lord" (Romans 8:38-39). Freedom in Christ transcends the physical conditions, the outer circumstances of one's life.

It is, to be sure, a freedom *from* — from fear, anxiety, legalism, self-indulgence. But it is also a freedom *for*, the freedom to be and to do, and that is what this book is about. The freedom to which Paul declares we are called in Jesus Christ has tremendous implications for faith and life. In the following pages I shall explore some of these implications, beginning with a chapter on the meaning of our call to freedom.

What follows is not an exposition but an extended application of the Galatians texts. Each of the chapters focuses on a particular aspect of our life in Christ, and, more broadly, of our human condition. The list of topics is wide-ranging but by no means exhaustive.

The questions at the end of each chapter are intended to encourage personal reflection and to facilitate group discussion. The uniqueness of the contents of this book is the application of the unifying theme of freedom to the various topics.

This is a devotional book. It reflects my personal faith in Christ and is written for people of faith. It is not an exercise in apologetics. It is rather a book on discipleship. I am writing as a believer to believers who want to become more faithful disciples of Jesus Christ.

It is also a book for thinkers, for Christianity is a thinking person's faith, as I shall try to show in Chapter 11. The paradoxical nature of faith is reflected in the seemingly antithetical topics of some of the chapters (e.g., our freedom to remember vs. our freedom to forget; our freedom to doubt vs. our freedom to be sure). It is my earnest hope that those who read this book will have a better understanding of and a deeper appreciation for their freedom in Christ and its implications for their daily lives.

Biblical quotations are usually from the New Revised Standard Version, occasionally from the Revised Standard Version, when the language is inclusive. I have not indicated which translation except when the distinction is needed for clarification. References for other quotations, when not indicated in the text, are included in the Endnotes.

In keeping with the nature and purpose of this study I have not discussed or attempted to debate any issues raised by historical biblical criticism, such as the authorship of the so-called "pastoral epistles." Though I am aware of the problems involved, I decided it would be easier for me and less confusing to my intended readers, when I quote from those epistles, simply to accept and not try to justify the traditional view that it was Paul who was writing to Timothy.

Once again I want to express my gratitude to Margie, my wife of more than half a century, for her perceptive comments, helpful suggestions, and incomparable proof-reading. Her encouragement has been a constant incentive to me throughout the years, as together we have learned what it means to be free in Christ.

Richard Stoll Armstrong
Princeton, New Jersey

Table Of Contents

Chapter One

Let Me Out Of Here!
Called To Freedom

As a lad of seven and a soon-to-be second grader at the boys military school where I had recently arrived, I experienced my share of the hazing to which new boys were invariably subjected. I remember being sent to the infirmary because I had "lobes on my ears," and being told to report to the Commandant because I had not been issued my keys to the oar locks.

These were harmless enough pranks to pull on a scared, gullible newcomer, who had never been separated from his parents before. But one evening that summer a group of older boys went too far. They forced me into a metal locker in the basement of our dormitory and informed me that they were going to leave me there — indefinitely! As they turned out the lights and noisily departed, I was instantly panic-stricken, fearing that I would be left there to die of suffocation. With my shoulders crammed tightly into that dark, stuffy, narrow, upright coffin, I was barely able to move my wrists enough to bang the backs of my hands against the sides of the locker. I began screaming at the top of my lungs, hoping that someone would hear me and come to my rescue, but knowing it was unlikely anyone would be in that part of the building at night.

Unbeknown to me, the boys who had put me there had quietly sneaked back in the dark to savor the success of their prank, which had certainly achieved the desired effect on their young victim. My terrified voice must have startled at least one of them, however, for he opened the locker and pulled me out. I never will forget the instant relief I felt when the door opened and I was released from that horrible tomb. My screams subsided into deep sobs, as they exacted a promise from me not to tell anyone what they had done.

11

I had nightmares about that horrible incident, and I'm sure that my present claustrophobic tendencies can be traced back to that summer night and what for me was a terrifying experience. I can't stand being confined, and without my present faith in God I could not make it through an MRI. Climbing up through the oppressively dank, dimly lit, tunnel-like passage of the Great Pyramid at Giza in Egypt, I suddenly panicked and had to retreat backwards on my hands and knees until I reached the open air. The thought of being in a straight jacket gives me the willies. I need freedom of move-ment. I hate being confined in any way. I get nervous when I'm in a crowded elevator.

Freedom means different things to different people. For one frightened little boy it meant being let out of a locker. To someone living under an oppressive dictatorship it would mean something else. For a teenager looking forward to turning twenty-one, it would mean something still different. Freedom is what most people would say they have whenever they are not restricted or confined in any way.

But if that is freedom, then who is really free? Obviously no one is free in that sense, for everyone is subject to all kinds of restrictions which limit and regulate one's freedom. There are the *laws of nature* to which we must conform or pay the penalty. Our bodies are not free from the necessity to eat and sleep.

There are the *laws of the state*, which also restrict our free-dom. We can't walk in and hold up a bank whenever we need money. We are not free to shoot people we don't like! There are also *eco-nomic* restrictions which limit our freedom: we can't have every-thing we want. We must be able to pay the price. Our income deter-mines where we live, how we travel, where we go, and what we do when we get there.

Then there are *occupational* restrictions. Everyone has to take orders from his or her superior authority. And those higher up are accountable to a board, or the electorate, or some other constitu-ency. There are *personal* limitations with which each individual must contend. Everyone has her or his mental, physical, and per-haps emotional limitations. There are also what might be called *circumstantial* restrictions, which also limit one's freedom — accidents, twists of fortune, family obligations over which one has no control.

And as if all these are not enough, we have also to reckon with endless social customs, mores, prejudices, and bigotries which erect further barriers to individual freedom. One slip of the tongue can be the downfall of a political candidate. An innocent hug can trigger a lawsuit for sexual harassment.

If freedom means the right to do whatever we want whenever we want, then we human beings are anything but free. Such freedom is a mirage, an illusive idea that many strive for but never fully attain, because there is no such thing as absolute freedom. It is always contingent and relative. It must be defined in terms of a particular condition.

It may be good or bad, noble or debased. It may be the earnest hope for political liberty, or the lust for uninhibited debauchery. The freedom of some college students to indulge in riotous living is far different from the freedom that Patrick Henry longed for, when he exclaimed, "Is life so dear or peace so sweet as to be purchased at the price of chains and slavery? Forbid it, Almighty God! I know not what course others may take, but as for me, give me liberty or give me death!"[1]

No matter how we define it, such freedom is limited freedom, and limited freedom is an oxymoron, a contradiction of terms. Limited freedom is not freedom at all. The freedom do to what we like, whether our intentions are honorable or degraded, is a false freedom, even when it is guaranteed by such a lofty statement as the Declaration of Independence, which declares that all people "are endowed by their Creator with certain unalienable rights, (and) that among these are life, liberty, and the pursuit of happiness."[2]

This freedom which we hold as an unalienable right we also cherish and use within the limits defined by law. But this is not the freedom of which the apostle Paul wrote, when he declared, "You were called to freedom, brothers and sisters" (Galatians 5:13a). The freedom to which we have been called is not political freedom, or economic freedom, or social freedom, or even moral freedom, but freedom of the spirit. It is the freedom which Jesus Christ bought for us with his life, a freedom to which all who accept him as their Lord and Savior are entitled. It is not something which we must struggle to attain. It is a gift of God, and it is proclaimed in the New Testament as a fact: "For freedom Christ has set us free" (Galatians 5:1a).

Christian freedom, however, is not freedom from restraint. It involves a new relationship with God in which we are free to do not what we want, but what we ought. Such freedom is not defined by laws; rather it is freedom *from* the law, as the New Testament proclaims, and thus from sin and the wages of sin, which is death (Romans 6:23). To be free from the law does not mean we need not obey the law of God, but rather that we need not depend upon our obedience to the law for our salvation. "For," said Paul, "a person is not justified by works of the law but through faith in Jesus Christ" (Galatians 2:16). To be free from sin does not mean that we are not sinful or that we never sin, but rather that through the death of Christ we have obtained forgiveness for our sins. To be free from death does not mean that we do not die but rather that nothing, not even death, can separate us from the love of God, which is in Christ Jesus our Lord (Romans 8:38-39).

To be free in the Christian sense, in short, means to recognize oneself to be a child of God. "For all who are led by the Spirit of God are children of God," wrote Paul to the Roman Christians. "...When we cry, 'Abba! Father!' it is that very Spirit bearing witness with our spirit that we are children of God, and if children, then heirs, heirs of God and joint heirs with Christ ... " (Romans 8:14-17b). A Christian is free to enjoy communion with God no matter what the external circumstances of one's life may be. Thus Paul knew himself to be free, even when he was standing in chains before King Agrippa. Roman law could not destroy that freedom. But Agrippa could not understand this. He saw only a prisoner in chains, and he said to Festus the governor, "This man could have been set free, if he had not appealed to Caesar" (Acts 26:32).

This man could have been set free! To which we, from our perspective, would want to reply, "Oh, how wrong you are, Agrippa! This man *is* free! Jesus Christ has set him free from all earthly bondage, so that he can say all things are his, for he belongs to

Christ, and Christ belongs to God!" (I Corinthians 3:21-23). It was Paul, in chains, who knew the secret of unlimited freedom. It was Paul, a prisoner for the Lord, who declared, "For freedom Christ has set us free; stand firm, therefore, and do not submit again to a yoke of slavery.... For you were called to freedom, brothers and sisters ... " (Galatians 5:1, 13a).

" ... only do not use your freedom as an opportunity for self-indulgence" (Galatians 5:13b). Our Christian freedom is a precious right, yet how often we misuse it, or abuse it, or neglect it. Even as we clamor for freedom, we take upon ourselves the yoke of slavery. We are in bondage to social custom, chained to the conventions of society, caught in the web of conformity. We have not always availed ourselves of our God-given freedom to be free!

Why? Is it fear — the fear of being unpopular, of being criticized, misunderstood, ridiculed, attacked? If we are afraid to be different, afraid to take a stand against the crowd for what we know is right, is that not a form of slavery? Are we not slaves to fear when we compromise our principles in order to avoid the unpleasant or unpopular consequences?

We talk about free will and the right to choose, but too often we measure that freedom by the standards of the world, instead of those of Christ. Jesus never intended freedom to mean the lack of obligation. We are truly free only as we conform to the spirit of Christ. Human beings were born to worship, and if we do not worship God, we will worship something else. To deny God is to declare one's allegiance to some idol.

When Moses came down from Mount Sinai bearing the tablets of stone, he found the people of Israel worshiping a golden calf. They had rejected Moses, forsaken their leader, even as he was communing with *Yahweh* on their behalf. They said to Aaron: "Come, make gods for us, who shall go before us; as for this Moses, the man who brought us up out of the land of Egypt, we do not know what has become of him" (Exodus 32:1b). So they forsook God and worshiped a golden calf!

It has ever been thus with humankind, including us. We are always tempted to forget God and turn to some idol of our own making. Intellectual agnostics believe themselves to be unencumbered by any religious superstition, but in reality are they not making a god of their own intellect? They are worshiping a golden calf called "reason." Militant nonbelievers worship themselves or something of their own creation or choice.

Those who reject Jesus Christ always erect some other kind of idol, whether it be money, or sex, or alcohol, or gambling, or easy living, or their profession, or their family, or some cause.

> *It's good when your heart has been gripped by a cause*
> *that calls for devotion and zeal.*
> *But if your cause blinds you to God's higher laws,*
> *how can you to God then appeal?*
> *No matter how worthy the cause you espouse,*
> *no matter how noble the goal,*
> *if gaining that end is the first of your vows,*
> *beware, lest you mortgage your soul!*[3]

To belong to Christ is perfect freedom. To belong to anyone or anything else (in the sense of being owned by it) is slavery.

The apostle Paul declared that we are saved by faith, not by our good works. We are not under law, but under grace. "What then?" he asked. "Should we sin because we are not under law but under grace? By no means!" (Romans 6:15). People have often misconstrued Paul's teaching, using it as a justification for indulging their "natural urges." But Paul makes it very clear that Christian freedom is not to be used as an excuse for unrighteous living. We must not confuse liberty with license. Some people do that when they use the famous maxim of St. Augustine to justify their self-indulgent behavior: "Love God and do as you please." It would be far better to say, "Love God and do as God pleases!"

Some insist that what we refer to as minor vices have nothing to do with one's relation to God. We are all sinners, so the argument goes; we all are recipients of God's grace, and no one needs to feel guilty, and certainly no one has a right to feel "holier than thou," simply because of one's personal habits. The argument is valid to a point, but not when it is used to justify turning liberty into license.

Such an attitude ignores Paul's strong admonition: "Do not use your freedom as an opportunity for the flesh." In other words, we are free *from* sin, but not free *to* sin. Be free, said Paul, "but through love become slaves to one another" (Galatians 5:13c). This is the paradox of Christian freedom. Peter said the same thing in his first letter: "As servants of God, live as free people, yet do not use your freedom as a pretext for evil" (I Peter 2:16).

"Thanks be to God," wrote Paul to the Romans, "that you having once been slaves of sin ... having been set free from sin, have become slaves of righteousness.... When you were slaves of sin, you were free in regard to righteousness.... But now that you have been freed from sin and enslaved to God, the advantage you get is sanctification. The end is eternal life" (Romans 6:17-18, 20-21).

Christian freedom is freedom to serve God, and we serve God in serving others. God has endowed us with free will. We are free to choose or to reject God. But the freedom to which we are called is found only in obedience to Christ, who came not to destroy the law but to fulfill it. The commandment in which all other laws find their meaning is the law of love. "You shall love the Lord your God with all your heart," said Jesus, "and with all your soul, and with all your strength, and with all your *mind*; and your neighbor as yourself" (Luke 10:27).

"Through love be servants of one another." Our failure to exercise our God-given freedom to be servants is the result of our not having discovered the basic truth that Christian freedom means service — not servitude but service. In the next chapter I shall discuss more thoroughly our freedom to serve; that is, why and how we are free to serve. For now I simply want to emphasize that to be called to freedom in Christ is to be called to serve. We cannot fulfill this calling by retreating into a spiritual shell. Our journey into the realm of faith is not a solo flight. Freedom does not mean rugged individualism. On the contrary, it means forgetting oneself for the sake of others and in so doing finding oneself. To be free is to be your neighbor's servant in love. As the mother is the slave of the infant at her breast, as the loving husband is the slave of his wife and she the willing slave of her husband, as a friend is a servant of his friends, so love makes willing slaves of us all, servants of one who came not to be served but to serve, and whose love was so great that he willingly and freely laid down his life for us.

Through freedom serve one another. We don't serve one another by indulging each other's vices. We don't serve one another by causing a brother or sister to stumble. We don't show our love by ignoring another's pain or needs. We don't serve Jesus Christ by forgetting him in public. We are called to freedom. We are no longer slaves to sin, no longer slaves to social pressures. If we believe in Christ, then we have the freedom which he purchased for us with his own life, freedom from the condemnation of our sin, freedom from anxiety, freedom from the fear of death. We are also free from despair, for we know that the future has meaning, because the future belongs to God and our times are in God's hands. We stand on the promises of God and claim our right to eternal fellowship with him through God's Son.

> *You were called to freedom, brothers and sisters . . .*
> *freedom from the worship of the idol of success;*
> *freedom from the bondage of the passion to possess;*
> *freedom from the conscience-binding pressure to conform;*
> *freedom from the selfish will's resistance to reform;*
> *freedom to embrace the truth, when others would deny it;*
> *freedom to defend the right, when others would defy it;*
> *freedom to be humble, when the world would make you proud;*
> *freedom to go God's way, caring not to please the crowd.*
>
> *And the truth will make you free. . .*
> *free to be a servant and yet call none other master;*
> *free to trust God's gracious will in triumph or disaster;*

*free to love your enemies and pray for those who curse
    you;*
free to give without expecting life to reimburse you;
*free, persuaded naught can separate you from God's
    love;*
*free, empowered by God's grace and wisdom from
    above;*
free, believing God can work for good in everything;
*free! — more than a conqueror, through Jesus Christ
    the King!⁴*

Questions For Personal Reflection And/Or Group Discussion

1. Have you ever experienced the feeling of being liberated or freed from something? What were the circumstances?

2. What conditions, if any, are restricting or confining you at present, and to what degree? How are you coping with those conditions?

3. This book assumes the reader will approach the various topics from her or his own faith perspective. How would you define the word "faith"? In a sentence or two how would you summarize your personal faith?

4. Freedom, as we have seen, means different things to different people. What does freedom mean to you?

5. This book wrestles with the meaning and implications of *Christian* freedom. What is your present understanding of what it means to be "free in Christ"?

6. How should a Christian respond to Christ's call to freedom? How have you responded? Are you really free?

Chapter Two

Can A Slave Be Free?
Free To Serve

"Through love become slaves to one another" (Galatians 5:13b).
The Revised Standard Version uses the word "servants" instead of
"slaves." The literal meaning of the Greek word *doulos* is "slave,"
but the RSV translators substituted a word which they must have
thought would be more understandable and acceptable to the modern mind.

It connotes the same idea, however, as evidenced by the fact
that there are those today who would like to eliminate entirely any
reference to servanthood in the proclamation of the gospel. Any
word suggestive of servitude is unacceptable to those whose ancestors may have experienced the evils of slavery, they argue. The
concept of the church as servant no longer communicates.

Although I abhor any form of human slavery, I disagree completely with those who want to discard the use of the concept of
Christian servanthood. There is no biblical or theological justification whatsoever for abolishing the servant image. The one text cited
by those who want to abandon the language of servanthood is taken
out of context from the passage in the Gospel of John where Jesus,
in his lengthy discourse, told his disciples, "I do not call you servants any longer, because the servant does not know what the master is doing; but I have called you friends, because I have made
known to you everything that I have heard from my Father" (John
15:15).

It is clear from what Jesus had said right before that saying
that the disciples' friendship with him was not one of equality. "You
are my friends," he declared in the preceding verse, *"if you do what
I command you"* (John 15:14). Jesus was preparing them for his
impending death. He charged them to love one another as he loved

21

them. The highest expression of friendship is one's willingness to die for one's friends. "No one has greater love than this, to lay down one's life for one's friends" (John 15:13). They were his friends, but they did not cease to be his servants. Nor did their being his servants prevent them from being his friends. To emphasize the point he would now call them friends, rather than servants, because he was sharing with them his heavenly secrets. Though he was still their Lord and Master and they his disciples, they were also his friends — and what a friend they had in Jesus!

The distinction Jesus made between a servant and a friend occurs nowhere else in the New Testament, although Luke in one place quotes Jesus' addressing the disciples as "my friends" (12:4). It is significant that the disciples referred to themselves consistently as "servants (slaves) of Christ." It was not "Paul, a friend of Jesus," but "Paul, a servant of Jesus Christ" writing to the church at Rome. It was not "James, a friend of Jesus" but "James, a slave of God and of the Lord Jesus Christ" (James 1:1). It was not "Simon Peter, a friend of Jesus," but "Simon Peter, a servant and apostle of Jesus Christ" (II Peter 1:1).

Nowhere in the New Testament does any disciple refer to himself as a friend of Jesus Christ. "This is how one should regard us," wrote Paul to the Corinthians, "as servants of Christ and stewards of the mysteries of God" (I Corinthians 4:1). And that is how all followers of Christ should consider themselves. So Paul urged the Philippians: "Let the same mind be in you that was in Christ Jesus, who, though he was in the form of God, did not regard equality with God as something to be exploited, but emptied himself, taking the form of a slave, being born in human likeness ... " (2:5-7).

To be in the mode and mold of Jesus Christ, then, is to be in the world as one who serves. By serving others we serve Christ, whom to serve is freedom, as Paul reminded the Galatians. The freedom to which we are called in Jesus Christ not only includes but is defined by our freedom to serve, and our Lord has given us an ideal example of what it means to be a servant. Jesus served others by ministering to their physical as well as to their spiritual needs. "He related to people where they were, as they were, while seeing what they could be and holding up to them the possibilities of a new and better life. He invited, but he did not insist. He challenged, but he did not coerce.... "[5]

As members of the body of Christ, therefore, we are called to be Christ's servants as well as his witnesses, both within and without the walls of the church. Remembering that the gospel of Jesus is a gospel of works as well as of deeds, our mission is to serve the world around us in whatever ways are needed, appropriate, and possible. That is what it means to be the servant people of God, who follow in the footsteps of one who came as a suffering servant. To be a disciple of Christ is to be a servant of Christ, and to be a servant of Christ is to be a servant of humanity.

Our English nouns "service" and "servant," and the verb "to serve" are used to translate several different Greek and Hebrew word groups, each with its own subtle distinction that is not apparent in the English translation. The Greek verb *douleuo* means to serve as a slave. "It refers to service that is not a matter of choice and implies complete dependence upon and total commitment to the owner or master (*kurios*). That explains Jesus' saying in the Sermon on the Mount, 'You cannot serve [as a slave] God and mammon' (Matthew 6:24), and Paul's statement, 'Do you not know that if you yield yourselves to any one as obedient slaves, you are slaves of the one whom you obey, either of sin, which leads to death, or of obedience, which leads to righteousness?'(Romans 6:16)."[6]

To be a slave of Christ, therefore, is to be freed from any other form of slavery. The freedom to which we are called in Christ means that we are no longer slaves to sin, to our passions and pleasures, to a legalistic code of conduct by which we have to prove our worthiness to God, or to anyone or anything else. Rather, because we are servants of Christ, we are free through love to be servants, willing servants, of one another.

Another important Greek word for servant is *diakonos*, which is someone who renders service. In the King James Version it is usually translated as "minister." It originally had to do with serving tables. The English transliteration is "deacon." It is the word Jesus used when he said, "Whoever would be great among you must be your servant" (Matthew 20:26; Mark 10:43). The verb form occurs in the passage already referred to: "The Son of Man came not to be served, but to serve" (Matthew 20:28 and Mark 10:45). Again, "I am among you as one who serves" (Luke 22:27).

The word *diakonos* has broad usage in the New Testament. The apostle Paul's comment that there are "varieties of service (diakonia) just as there are varieties of spiritual gifts" (I Corinthians 12:5) is a reminder that there are any number of ways that you and I through love can serve Christ and one another. We need to identify our individual gifts and discover ways to use them in Christ's service. What better context is there for recognizing, celebrating, and utilizing one anther's gifts than in the community of faith, one's local church? We need to be about that task every day in order to help one another fulfill our calling to be Christ's servants.

Being a servant of Christ, however, is not just a matter of doing occasional good deeds. It's not just what we do, but how we feel about what we do. It's not just doing service, but being a servant. It has more to do with attitude than with activity. We're not being servants when we do things with a patronizing, or condescending, or self-serving attitude. We're not being servants when we expect to be rewarded for what we do, or when there are ulterior motives behind our good deeds. Jesus made this crystal clear in his response to the disciples after James and John came to him asking for privileged places in his kingdom. The other disciples were angry with James and John for beating them to the punch, and Jesus's response to them suggests the qualities that should define a true servant of Christ:

> *You know that among the Gentiles those whom they recognize as their rulers lord it over them, and their great ones are tyrants over them. But it is not so among you; but whoever wishes to become great among you must be your servant, and whoever wishes to be first among you must be slave of all. For the Son of Man came not to be served but to serve, and to give his life a ransom for many* (Mark 10:41-45).

The first obvious quality is humility, the willingness to lose oneself. It is the opposite of the attitude displayed by those who like to lord it over others. It is to be content with anonymity, to serve without thought of reward, without worrying about who gets the credit, without expecting to be thanked. It is to be unselfconscious in one's concern for serving others.

Don't think too highly of yourself, warns the apostle Paul. In true humility one thinks not of oneself at all.[7]

The truly humble person does not shout to the world, "Look what I've done!" or "See what I'm doing!" but receives the respect of those whose admiration true humility always inspires.

The second quality implied in Jesus response is sensitivity; that is, sensitivity to human need. One cannot serve others if one is not aware of their needs, their hopes and fears, their pain and sorrow, their sickness and suffering. "Are you able to drink the cup that I drink?" (Mark 10:38). Can we feel Jesus' concern for the sins of the world, his compassion for the lost and the lonely, the sick and the sorrowing, the poor and the oppressed, his love for the unlovable? Worthy servants are sensitive to their Master's moods, and they share their Master's feelings for others.

Sensitivity must lead not just to sentimentality, but to obedient action. Obedience is the third quality of a true servant of Christ, obedience expressed in deeds, not just feelings or words. Taking the form of a slave, Jesus "humbled himself and became obedient to the point of death — even death on a cross" (Philippians 2:5-7).

We must not be like the Romanticists whose sentimentality often carried them to cruel extremes, such as putting a wild bird in a cage so they could weep over its pitiful efforts to escape. The Romanticists were playing with emotion, dabbling in sentiment. That's not the way Christ expects to be served. It's not enough to feel sorry for the underprivileged; one must express one's concern in action, with whatever deeds of mercy are called for, in whatever way the circumstances will allow.

I remember a young doctor in a church I served in Philadelphia. One Sunday morning the Holy Spirit stirred his heart with a desire to help some underprivileged native Americans. That summer he served for six weeks as a non-paid member of the medical staff at the Ganado Mission in Arizona. Another couple, who were both teachers, took a two-year leave of absence to serve as fraternal workers in Africa.

An elderly man approached me after church one Sunday and said he was too old to be a good worker for the church, but he realized he could do much more than he had been doing to support it financially, and he increased his giving dramatically.

In each of these instances concern had led to action. That's the way it works with servants of Christ. They see a need, and in obedience to the prompting of the Holy Spirit they do what they can to help meet it. Servants are obedient to their master, always be ready to respond to the call of Christ whenever it comes and wherever it may lead. Where it leads us to go and what it leads us to do may not be where we want to go or what we want to do.

That reality points to one more quality required of a servant of Christ: courage. It takes courage, because serving Christ can lead to conflict. We may not have to drink the same cup that Jesus drank, or be baptized with the baptism with which he was baptized, which was his death on the cross. But the life to which Christ calls us is no bed of roses. The path of service may lead through personal deprivation, pain, and suffering, perhaps even death, as it has for countless Christians across the centuries and throughout the world. If we're obedient to Christ we cannot escape conflict with those whose life-style and values are threatened by our attitudes and actions. Every time we take a stand for truth and justice, the forces of bigotry and prejudice, corruption and greed will be quick to attack.

Often it takes a crisis of some kind to separate the sheep from the goats. During the racial upheavals of the 1960s (I remember those struggles as if they were yesterday) some members of the church I was serving took seriously Paul's affirmation that "there is no longer Jew or Greek, there is no longer slave or free, there is no longer male and female; for all of you are one in Christ Jesus" (Galatians 3:28). They would have added "there is no longer black or white." They took their stand against friends and even members of their own family who resented and were resisting the church officers' determination to be an inclusive congregation in a racially changing community. Those who were struggling to be faithful to what they knew in their heart Christ would have them do, discovered that Christ's way is not the popular way. At the heart of our faith there is a cross![8]

These, then, are four essential qualities of a true servant of Christ: humility, sensitivity, obedience, courage. There are others, to be sure, but these four are basic to Christian servanthood. They describe the attitude of those who are free to serve. We realize, of course, that each of us has these qualities only to a relative and limited degree. No one is perfect. No one is as humble and sensitive and obedient and courageous as one ought to be, all the time, if ever. If we think we are, we are no longer humble! Humility is an elusive quality: the moment you think you've got it, you've lost it!

But here again is the amazing paradox of our freedom in Christ. It is in the awareness of our inadequacies that our worthiness is to be found, for our worthiness is not in ourselves but in Christ. The measure of our worthiness is not our own self-evaluation or anyone else's evaluation of our humility, sensitivity, obedience, and courage; rather it is our willingness to serve. It is our desire to be servants despite our unworthiness, because of the worthiness imputed to us by our Lord Jesus Christ. That's the paradox. It is in losing ourselves that we find ourselves, and it is in becoming his slave that we are freed from all forms of human bondage. Because we are servants of Christ, we are free through love to serve others. For a servant of Christ that is not servitude, but joyful service.

Those whom we regard as leaders of the church, such as pastors, church leaders, and denominational executives, have to remember that they, too, are servants of Christ and his church. It is very easy for those in positions of power and influence to forget that. Denominational executives can be tempted to act like bureaucratic bigwigs, instead of realizing they are called to be servants of the servants.

Christian leadership is not an exercise of power, but a rendering of service. That is why the constitution of my own denomination uses the term *servant* leadership. It describes a style of leadership that is characterized not by coercion but by persuasion, not by exaction but by example, not by force but by faith.

Servant leaders and servant followers alike are called to freedom, including the freedom through love to serve one another. This, then, is how we should regard ourselves, as servants of our Lord Jesus Christ, whom to know is life, whom to love is joy, whom to serve is perfect freedom.

John Bode's familiar hymn could be a theme song for servants of Christ in any age:

> *O Jesus, I have promised to serve thee to the end;*
> > *be thou forever near me, my Master and my Friend.*
> *I shall not fear the battle, if thou art by my side,*
> > *nor wander from the pathway, if thou wilt be my Guide.*
> *O Jesus, thou hast promised to all who follow thee*
> > *that where thou art in glory there shall thy servant be.*
> *And, Jesus, I have promised to serve thee to the end;*
> > *O give me grace to follow, my Master and my Friend!*[9]

Questions For Personal Reflection And/Or Group Discussion

1. How do you feel about the use of the term "servant" to describe one's role as a Christian?

2. Do you see yourself as a servant of Jesus Christ? How would you describe your servanthood?

3. What kinds of things keep you from being a more faithful servant of Christ?

4. What qualities in addition to those mentioned define for you a true servant of Christ?

5. When have you come closest to being a true servant? What were the circumstances? Did you experience a sense of freedom at the time?

6. Where does the church fit into your servanthood?

Chapter Three

Why Be A Noisy Gong?
Free To Love

In the preceding chapter we discussed our freedom to serve. Since it is through love that we serve one another, it is appropriate that we look next at how our freedom in Christ informs our understanding of Christian love.

One might immediately ask, Is there anything to be said about love that has not already been said by poets, bards, and sages of every realm and every age? The lyrical soul has ever poured out its testimonies to love, "that golden key that opes the palace of eternity."[10] "Mightier far than strength of nerve and sinew, or the sway of magic potent over sun and star is love," said Wordsworth,[11] "And when Love speaks," wrote Shakespeare, "the voice of all the gods makes heaven drowsy with the harmony."[12]

Most of us have neither the grace nor wit to pen such exquisite lines as these. Yet we do know what love is, and we know that without love, life is meaningless and barren. It is love that makes the world go round, as one songster put it. "The mind has a thousand eyes, and the heart but one; yet the light of a whole life dies, when love is done."[13]

We also know that there is within us a capacity for loving, a need for *giving* love, an innate desire that must be satisfied if we are to be truly happy. How many suicide notes bear the desperate and tragic signatures of those utterly lonely souls who felt they had no one to love.

There may be despair in love, and sorrow, as when love is unrequited. There may be disappointment and pain, as when love's object proves unworthy. But despite these hazards, to love and to be loved are beautiful requisites of nature, without which we would indeed be less than human.

I hold it true, whate'er befall,
I feel it, when I sorrow most;
'Tis better to have loved and lost
Than never to have loved at all.[14]

There are, of course, various expressions love: love of friends, love of family, love of animals, love of country, love for an object or an activity or a cause, love of God. Each one is unique, with its own distinctive characteristics and expressions, and even within these general classifications there are different degrees and kinds of love. Under love of family, for example, the love between a husband and wife is different from that between father and son. A mother's love for her daughter is different from a daughter's love for her mother. Indeed, no two loves are exactly alike. Every relationship is unique because it involves two unique individuals.

The ancient Greeks allowed for some of these distinctions by using several different words to represent various kinds of love. Whereas they distinguished between sexual love, and family love, and brotherly love, and social love, we have only the one word "love" to express everything from the basic aspects of sexual desire to the lofty pinnacles of unselfish devotion.

Herein lies our difficulty, for our English word "love" does not connote the same qualities that are conveyed by the Greek word which the apostle Paul used in the magnificent hymn on love which he wrote to the Corinthians. Paul used the word *agape*, which is the principle New Testament word for love. It was the term applied to the wholly free and uncaused love God extends to human beings — spontaneous, unselfish, unmerited, voluntary, grace-filled love. Our love for other human beings is an extension of this love and is totally dependent upon it. "We love, because (God) first loved us" (I John 4:19).

Without this love, this *agape*, nothing else matters. Whatever spiritual gifts we may possess apart from love mean nothing. This is the point Paul makes so eloquently in I Corinthians:

If I speak in the tongues of mortals and of angels, but do not have love, I am a noisy gong or a clanging cymbal.

And if I have prophetic powers, and understand all mys-
teries and all knowledge, and if I have all faith, so as to
remove mountains, but do not have love, I am nothing. If I
give away all my possessions, and if I hand over my body
so that I may boast, but do not have love, I gain nothing
(13:1-3).

In other words, everything which we are accustomed to call "love" may not be Christian love at all. The ability to speak in tongues is nothing without love. Faith that can move mountains, even the willingness to die a martyr's death means nothing apart from *agape*. We would never even know what true love is, if God had not revealed it to us. For God *is* love. *God* is love, and no one can know God except by God's self-revelation.

But the stupendous fact of our Christian faith is that God *did* reveal God's own self, God's nature, in the person of Jesus Christ. "God's love was revealed among us in this way: God sent the only Son into the world so that we might live through him" (I John 4:9). Everything the New Testament has to say about *agape*, then, is summarized and expressed in Jesus Christ, who is God's love, God's *agape*, revealed. Jesus exemplifies all of the noble qualities which Paul attaches to *agape* in I Corinthians 13. These are the qualities of true love, the love of those in whom the spirit of Christ dwells.

When I speak of our freedom to love, I mean this kind of love, none other. Not the love which Plutarch, the Greek moralist, called the holiest right of the soul, however exalted he envisioned it. Not the freedom to love another member of the opposite sex, or the same sex, which is hardly an unused freedom. Not the freedom to love a friend or a relative, which only a misanthrope would fail to exercise. Not the freedom to love one's country, or one's college, or one's dog. I mean the freedom to love as God loves us, the freedom to express *agape* in all these other relationships. In Jesus Christ we are called to freedom, and that includes the freedom to love God! "What is the chief end of man?" asked the first question of the Westminster Shorter Catechism long before inclusive language became a concern. "Man's chief end is to love God and to enjoy him forever," was the answer confirmands had to memorize.

But why speak of our loving God as a *freedom*? Because the capacity to love God is a gift of God, a gift which God freely offers to all humankind. Every *normal* human being has the capacity to love God; it is an essential part of our humanity. God has endowed us with the ability to respond to God's love. And you can be sure that those unfortunate souls who may not have been born with that capacity are loved just as much by God.

I say every *normal* person has the capacity to love, and every person has the *duty* to love, for the commandment to love our neighbor is for all humankind. So is the promise that whoever abides in love abides in God, for God *is* love (I John 4:16b).

Yes, the freedom to love is a sacred right, but alas, it is for many of us an unused right. And because it is, that which we often call "love" is not true love at all. "Love," said Paul, "is patient and kind." We love our children and grandchildren, but are we always patient and kind? "Love is not jealous or boastful." We love our friends, but are we never jealous of them? Do we never boast, inwardly if not outwardly? "Love is not arrogant or rude." We cherish our religion, but are we always tactful in talking to others about it? Have we never been arrogant about our political views, or rude about our pet peeves?

"Love does not insist on its own way." Are we not usually looking out for ourselves, demanding our rights, insisting on our getting what's coming to us, our fair share? "Love is not irritable or resentful." How often we nurse our hurt feelings, harbor our need to be vindicated. How quick we often are to take offense. Just watch the way people drive in traffic! How often children sulk when their parents refuse a request. Brothers and sisters squabble and squawk. Husbands and wives nitpick, needle, and nag, and life in many homes is a constant verbal free-for-all.

"Love does not rejoice at wrong, but rejoices in the right." Yet how much we delight in juicy gossip, in hearing a rival's reputation smeared. How tempted we are to rejoice in the mistakes and sins of others, instead of rejoicing in the right. *Agape* is slow to suspect, quick to forgive, willing to accept excuses, eager to hear an explanation for a wrong. "Loves bears all things, believes all thing, hopes all things, endures all things."

True love hallows every relationship. It prevents the distortions which other loves may display. I remember a couple who having one child, wanted no more, because, as they put it, "our love for our son is so great that we can't bear to think of having to share it with another child. We have only so much love to give, and we want to give it all to him." They had forgotten the marvelous elasticity of the human heart. "True love," said the poet Shelley, "in this differs from gold and clay, that to divide is not to take away."[15]

When we use our God-given freedom to love, other loves take on a new luster. The love of a friend for a friend is stronger, kinder, deeper. Like David's love for Jonathon; their friendship was a covenant made with God as their witness. Or Tennyson's love for Arthur Henry Hallam, to whom he wrote his immortal poem, *In Memoriam.*

So, too, the love between parent and child, or between brother and sister, is more beautiful. So, too, the love between a man and a woman, than which there is no lovelier love in the entire realm of human affection, becomes a pure and holy expression of God's love. Like the love of Elizabeth Barrett for Robert Browning:

> *How do I love thee? Let me count the ways.*
> *I love thee to the depth and breadth and height*
> *my soul can reach, when feeling out of sight*
> *for ends of Being and ideal Grace.*
> *I love thee to the level of everyday's*
> *most quiet need, by sun and candlelight.*
> *I love thee freely, as men strive for Right;*
> *I love thee purely, as they turn from Praise.*
> *I love thee with passion put to use*
> *in my old griefs, and with my childhood's faith.*
> *I love thee with a love I seemed to lose*
> *with my lost saints —I love thee with the breath,*
> *smiles, tears, of all my life! —and, if God choose,*
> *I shall but love thee better after death."[16]*

Love like this is possible only because God is love. There have been great loves apart from any knowledge of Jesus Christ, of course, like Mark Anthony's love for Cleopatra. But however deep the affection which led Anthony to kill himself when told of Cleopatra's supposed death, it was not the love of which Paul wrote. However touching the fictional love of Romeo for Juliet, or Cyrano for the beautiful Roxanne, they are pale beside the love of God in Christ.

When we have encountered this love, the "love that wilt not let us go," we know what true love is. When we have this love, all other love takes on new meaning and new purpose. Other loves become expressions of the love of Christ in us. When one has experienced the love of Christ, one responds by giving to others that same kind of love, never perfectly, to be sure, but always striving toward perfection. Thus love for one's fellow human beings is the fruition of God's love for us, and the proof of our love for God.

But our love for God is still different from God's love, because while God's love is spontaneous and uncaused, ours comes only in response to God's prior love for us. If we sincerely want to love God more, then we need to open our hearts to God's love as we have seen it expressed in Jesus Christ. We have to let Christ's love fill our lives, so that we can share it with others. This is how we express our love for him. And to love Christ is the noblest virtue we can possess, the most precious freedom we have as human beings. This freedom to love God in and through Christ is the apex of our humanity, our most glorious characteristic, the one which, more than any other, distinguishes us from all other creatures. Animals can have a kind of love for other animals and for human beings, but only we human beings can love God with heart, soul, mind, and strength.

Yet there are and always have been those who would scoff at such a statement. The Greek philosopher Aristotle, for example, argued that it makes no more sense to speak of loving God, or of being loved by God, than it does to speak of being loved by a lifeless object.[17]

Aristotle was a great philosopher, but he did not know the God we have come to know in and through Jesus Christ. No one has ever seen God, that is true. But whoever has seen the Son, has seen the Father (John 14:9). "The Son, who is in the bosom of the Father, he has made him known" (John 1:18). "He has brought light and immortality to light through the gospel" (II Timothy 1:10).

Our freedom to love, to respond to the eternal love of God in Jesus Christ, is founded on our faith that he has come. It issues in our hope that he will come again. Our faith is the foundation on which our hope is based, and our love for him is the current expression of both. Faith looks back; hope looks ahead; loves dwells in the present. Love is faith and hope in action. Love is always active. It is not an abstract idea but a dynamic reality that, like faith and hope, cannot be destroyed. Knowledge, prophecy, all other spiritual gifts will pass away, but faith, hope, and love will always remain, because God is love, and God is eternal.

> *Love never ends. But as for prophecies, they will come to an end; as for tongues, they will cease; as for knowledge, it will come to an end. For we know only in part, and we prophesy only in part; but when the complete comes, the partial will come to an end. When I was a child, I spoke like a child, I thought like a child, I reasoned like a child; when I became an adult, I put an end to childish ways. For now we see in a mirror, dimly, but then we will see face to face. Now I know only in part; then I will know fully, even as I have been fully known. And now faith, hope, and love abide, these three; and the greatest of these is love* (I Corinthians 13:8-13).

Questions For Personal Reflection
And/Or Group Discussion

1. Explain in your own words the relationship between Christian freedom and our love for God.

2. How do you understand the expression, "God is love." If God is love, does that mean Love is God? (If A = B, does not then B = A?)

3. How has your knowledge of Jesus Christ informed or influenced your faith in and love for God?

4. Can you think of examples from your own experience of the kind of love the Apostle Paul describes in I Corinthians 13 (*agape*)?

5. What would it mean for you to love God with all your heart, soul, mind, and strength? What would have to be different?

6. What are the barriers that keep you from loving your neighbor as Christ commanded?

Chapter Four

Who's On The Throne?
Free To Give

Is Christianity really a religion of love? Most of us who call ourselves Christians would be quick to say it is, but do we live as if it is? We are not likely to unless and until we understand that Christian faith is a faith that gives.

If the freedom to which we have been called in Jesus Christ includes the freedom to love, it must also include the freedom to give. For a Christian it is a three-dimensional kind of giving. That is to say, there are three steps required to experience and appropriate our Christian freedom to give.

The first step is *giving up*. Our Judeo-Christian faith begins with the recognition that to worship anything less than God is idolatry. If I am unwilling to give up that which has become for me an idol, whatever it may be — money, alcohol, drugs, sex, success, security, revenge, my job, my career, my hobby, my recreation, my country, my family, myself —if anything else has become more important to me than God, then I have denied the faith I profess.

Who sits on the throne of your heart? Anything less than God, good or bad, is an idol. God and God alone is worthy of our utmost devotion, our complete loyalty, our total trust. No cause, no person, no-thing can take God's place. Jesus demands our complete loyalty. "Whoever comes to me and does not hate father and mother, wife and children, brothers and sisters, yes, and even life itself, cannot be my disciple," he said (Luke 14:26).

That's a hard saying, any way you look at it. Jesus did not mean, of course, that we should not love our families. That would be contrary to everything he taught and represented in his own life. What he must have meant was that our love for another person, including our own family, cannot displace our love of God, that our love of family must be expressed in the context of our love for God. Even so, it is a hard saying, because there are times when it is difficult to know how to put God first in relation to family obligations. Honor your father and mother, says the 5th Commandment. We honor God when we keep that commandment. "Husbands, love your wives," instructed Paul (Ephesians 5:25). It's not a choice between loving God and loving one's family, but of loving one's family in a way that honors God.

In the first chapter the point was made that even one's noblest cause can become an idol, if it usurps the place of Christ, including the cause of freedom. In terms of our human spirituality, the idol of personal independence is for many people the hardest of all to renounce. They go on feathering their nests, building their own security systems, locking God out of all or part of their lives. They either have not recognized or have refused to acknowledge their dependence upon the Divine Creator and Ruler of the universe, the Source and Sustainer of all life, the Giver of every good and perfect gift. The first step toward becoming a Christian involves giving up the notion that you are the general manager of the universe. It means knowing that you are not the master of your fate and the captain of your soul, notwithstanding William Ernest Henley's well-known poem, which many of us had to memorize in school.[18]

But to admit that takes more humility than many of us have. In an age that glorifies self-assertion, we think and act as if we are in complete control of our lives, until we are jolted out of our complacency by the discovery that we have a terminal illness, or by the unexpected death of a loved one, or by some other calamity. "Come now," wrote James, "you who say, 'Today or tomorrow we will go to such and such a town and spend a year there, doing business and making money.' Yet you do not even know what tomorrow will bring. What is your life? For you are a mist that appears for a little while and then vanishes. Instead you ought to say, 'If the Lord wishes, we will live and do this or that.' As it is, you boast in your arrogance; all such boasting is evil" (James 4:13-16).

A faith that gives must first *give up*, and then it must *give in*. Giving up means renouncing all idols; giving in for a Christian mean surrendering to Jesus Christ. Giving up requires confession;

giving in requires commitment. Giving up means acknowledging one's need of a Savior; giving in means accepting him as the Lord of your life. "If any want to become my followers," said Jesus,"let them deny themselves and take up their cross and follow me" (Matthew 16:24).

People of other faiths wonder how we Christians can talk about God and Jesus in the same breath. Non-believers wonder how we can talk about God at all. It is an epistemological question, to which people of faith should be prepared to give an answer. How can we know God, if, as John's Gospel forthrightly states, "No one has ever seen God" (1:18a)? But John immediately added, "It is God the only Son, who is close to the Father's heart, who has made him known" (1:18b).

The implication of John's message for us today is, therefore, if you want to know what God is like, get to know Jesus. He has shown us what God has done for us, and what God expects of us, and what God can do for us. As Paul declared, "He has brought life and immortality to light through the gospel" (II Timothy 1:10).

Muslims, Jews, and Christians all worship the same God, though we know God by different names and in different ways. There is only one God, who, as the writer of the Book of Hebrews points out, revealed himself in many and various ways in the days of old. "But in these last days he has spoken to us by a Son, whom he appointed heir of all things, through whom he also created the worlds. He is the reflection of God's glory and the exact imprint of God's very being ... " (Hebrews 1:2-3).

Christians believe, therefore, that the world has been given a fuller understanding, indeed the ultimate revelation of God, in Jesus Christ, who in some mysterious way that defies our human understanding was himself the very incarnation of God, fully divine and yet fully human. So Jesus could say, "I and the Father are one (John 10:30).... Whoever has seen me has seen the Father" (John 14:9). Christians affirm that in Christ God was reconciling the world to himself (II Corinthians 5:19), and that through his life, death, resurrection, and ascension Christ has provided for all who accept him a unique way, and the only way, of salvation. He knew this about himself, and therefore could boldly claim, "I am the way, and the truth, and the life; no one comes to the Father but by me" (John 14:6).

Jesus tried to prepare his disciples for his eventual arrest, execution, and resurrection, but they were slow of understanding. They didn't get the message. But Jesus had also promised them that although he would no longer be with them in the flesh, he would not leave them comfortless, for he would send the Holy Spirit to be with them forever, whom the unbelieving world cannot receive, because it neither sees him nor knows him (John 14:17). But the Holy Spirit, "whom the Father will send in my name," said Jesus, "will teach you everything, and remind you of all that I have said to you. . . He will bear witness to me. . He will glorify me, for he will take what is mine and declare it to you" (John 14:26, 15:26, 16:14).

Thus it is the Holy Spirit who enables us to grasp the truth of Jesus' words. When the light dawns and we are able to accept Christ for who he is, that is the work of the Holy Spirit. It is the Spirit bearing witness in our hearts to the truth of Jesus' words, exactly as Jesus promised.

Christian faith is faith in Jesus Christ, who is "the pioneer and perfecter of our faith" (Hebrews 12:2). We have no right to call ourselves Christians until we surrender our lives to him. A faith that gives is a faith that gives up all idols and gives in to Jesus Christ.

Yet it cannot stop there, for Christian faith is also a faith that *gives out* for others. "I am the true vine," said Jesus, "and my Father is the vine grower. He removes every branch in me that bears no fruit. Every branch that bears fruit he prunes to make it bear more fruit" (John 15:1-2). We are called to bear fruit for the kingdom of God, the fruit of good works. That's the warrant for our freedom to give out. "By this my Father is glorified," Jesus went on to say, "that you bear much fruit, and so prove to be my disciples" (John 15:8).

Our words and deeds are the expressions of our faith. Giving up requires confession; giving in requires commitment; giving out requires compassion. How we treat our fellow human beings is the test of our loyalty to Jesus Christ, who said that what we do or fail to do for others, we do or fail to do for him (Matthew 25:40,45). When we give to some worthy charity in Jesus' name, we are giving to him. When we help a struggling sister or brother, we do it for Christ. When we serve on some worthy community project that is helping to meet human need, we are serving Christ. When we give sacrificially to our church we are giving to Christ.

You might be thinking, What about those who have little or nothing to give to others? Shut-ins, for example, and people who can no longer get about, what do they have to give? Their prayers, if nothing else.

> *If the shut-ins all united*
> *in one voice of common prayer,*
> *what a ceaseless shower of blessing*
> *would be falling everywhere!*
> *Though so weak, and oft-times helpless,*
> *they can wield a mighty power,*
> *lifting up their soul's petition*
> *to the Savior, hour by hour.*
> *Never soldier in fierce conflict*
> *could a higher honor bring*
> *than the shut-in who's performing*
> *"secret service" for the King.*[19]

Whenever we give out for others, performing acts of mercy, justice, compassion, and love, we are bearing fruit for the kingdom. It is Christ who frees us and empowers us to do that. "Abide in me as I abide in you," Jesus told his disciples. "Just as the branch cannot bear fruit by itself unless it abides in the vine, neither can you unless you abide in me. I am the vine, you are the branches. Those who abide in me and I in them bear much fruit, because apart from me you can do nothing" (John 15:4-5).

We have to give up and give in before we can give out. Otherwise, we could become the kind of people who resent being asked to give to any worthy cause, though they never respond to any appeal; or who refuse to pledge to their church, though they expect their church to have a budget and do things in a business-like manner; or who pledge very little, though they have very much compared to people in many parts of the world, the poorest of the poor, like those I have seen in parts of Africa.

It is Jesus Christ who frees us to give as Paul urged the Corinthians to give, "not reluctantly or out of compulsion, for God loves a cheerful giver" (II Corinthians 9:7). If our giving is to be a willing gift rather than an exaction, it must be prompted by the love of Christ, who cuts us loose from the chains of selfishness and frees us to give out to others, joyfully and sacrificially.

That is exactly what happened to Zacchaeus after he met Jesus (see Luke 19:1-10). Anyone who attended Sunday School growing up knows the story of Zacchaeus, the tax collector, who, because he was short of stature, climbed up into a sycamore tree to get a better look at Jesus, who was passing through Jericho.

It would be difficult for Americans, even those of us who have had the unpleasant experience of being audited by the I.R.S., to imagine how unpopular the tax collectors were in Jesus' time. Unlike today, collecting taxes under the Roman government was a business. Individuals would buy the right to collect taxes in a given province, district, or town, and contract with the Roman government to pay so much money into the public treasury. The actual collections were made by sub-ordinates, who in turn paid for the privilege. In return for the risk and labor involved it was understood that the tax collectors would keep for themselves a fraction of what was paid them.

Apparently there was no way to prevent their cut from becoming too large, with the result that extortion was the common practice among the tax collectors. The fact that the tax collectors were usually from the native population only added to their unpopularity, especially among the Jews, who looked upon the Jewish tax gatherers as traitors, agents of a heathen government, and tools of a foreign power they hated. Tax collectors, therefore, were social outcasts, unfit company for any loyal Jew to associate with.

Such a man was Zacchaeus, who we are told was a chief tax collector, and rich, which means he was an extortioner like all the rest. As chief of the Jericho I.R.S., he had a good thing going. What a shock it must have been to the crowd, therefore, not to mention

44

the surprise to Zacchaeus himself, when Jesus spotted him in the tree and said, "Zacchaeus, hurry and come down, for I must stay at your house today." The little man climbed down at once and received Jesus joyfully, as the crowd murmured, "He has gone in to be the guest of a sinner!"

Luke does not tell us what went on in the house. We only know the before and the after. Whatever transpired inside, one thing we do know: Zacchaeus was a changed man when he came out! He said, "Look, half of my possessions, Lord, I will give to the poor; and if I have defrauded anyone of anything, I will pay back four times as much." He obviously had given up the idol he had worshiped all his life.

Zacchaeus had been living strictly for Zacchaeus. Like all those whose purse is their god, he could never have enough. Wealth could not ease the pain of loneliness. He couldn't be happy, knowing others hated him. While he cheated them out of their money, he was cheating himself out of life.

How do we account for his radical transformation? There is only one answer: Jesus Christ. Nothing happens to a person's giving until something first happens to the person. All his life Zacchaeus had been trying to get; now he wanted to give. And his first gift was the gift of his heart to Jesus Christ. When one gives in to Christ, it shows. In Zacchaeus' case, the immediate evidence of his change of heart was his desire to give out to others. He not only gave half of his wealth to the poor, he also righted his wrongs by restoring fourfold all that he had wrongfully taken.

Zacchaeus discovered that true happiness is to be found not in getting, but in giving. This is a lesson we should not have to be taught, for anyone who has ever loved another person, knows the joy of giving. But it is in the context of our Christian faith that this lesson finds its deepest meaning. When Zacchaeus declared his intention to share his wealth with the poor and to restore fourfold anything he had wrongfully taken, Jesus said, "Today salvation has come to this house."

In Jesus Christ we are called to freedom, and Zacchaeus, like Paul himself, is a beautiful reminder that the freedom to which we are called includes our being freed to give. It is a freedom which we can easily neglect, if we do not continue to lean on Christ. Apart from Jesus Christ I know I would quickly resort to my old selfish ways. Apart from Christ we are not likely to love our enemies, do good to those who hate us, bless those who curse us, and pray for those who abuse us, as he commanded his disciples to do (Luke 6:27-28). Those who commit vengeful acts of terrorism or who participate in violent demonstrations for their cause are certainly not prompted by the spirit of Christ, of whom the apostle Peter wrote, "When he was abused, he did not return abuse; when he suffered, he did not threaten; but he entrusted himself to the one who judges justly" (1 Peter 2:23).

There is no way one can hope to follow Christ's example without his help, but as Paul declared in that great affirmation of faith I have quoted elsewhere in this book, "I can do all things in him who strengthens me!" (Philippians 4:13).[20] Before his conversion Paul's self-identity had been wrapped up in his own righteousness under the law, which he expressed in his zealous persecution of the Christians. The law was his idol. But he gave it up and gave in to Christ, and he spent the rest of his life giving out for others. Zacchaeus, like Paul, had discovered what it means to be free to give.

We give thee but thine own,
*   whate'er the gift may be;*
all that we have is thine alone,
*   a trust, O Lord, from thee.*

To comfort and to bless,
*   to find a balm for woe,*
to tend the lone and fatherless,
*   is angels' work below.*

The captive to release,
*   to God the lost to bring,*
to teach the way of life and peace
*   — it is a Christlike thing.*

And we believe thy word,
*   though dim our faith may be;*
whate'er for thine we do, O Lord,
*   we do it unto thee.*[21]

Questions For Personal Reflection And/Or Group Discussion

1. How do you understand Jesus' saying "Whoever comes to me and does not hate father and mother, wife and children, brothers and sisters, yes, and even life itself, cannot be my disciple"?

2. What kinds of things keep some people you know and care about from committing their lives to Jesus Christ? Can you think of any barriers that stand in the way of your own total commitment?

3. What do you think about Jesus' claim "no one comes to the Father but by me"? What about people of other faiths?

4. What is your understanding of the role of the Holy Spirit in one's faith pilgrimage?

5. Is your charitable giving a good measure of your Christian faith? How do you see the relationship between Christian freedom and giving?

6. Would you say you have experienced the joy of giving? When and how?

Chapter Five

This Is The Life!
Free To Live

I remember a scene from a science fiction thriller I saw on television in which some doctors were baffled by a man whose pulse, blood pressure, breathing, everything about him, indicated he should be dead. But he wasn't. "It's impossible," they said. "Medical science says this man is dead. But he's alive."

Fantastic? Yes, but truth is stranger than fiction, for there are millions of persons who have all the indications of being alive, but they are not really living at all. George Bernard Shaw suggested an epitaph for such people: "Died at thirty; buried at sixty."

Life is a gift; *living* is an art. All of us are alive, but not all of us are living. Most people feel they are really living when they're spending their time in ways that to them are immensely enjoyable. For some people it means having beer and pretzels while watching a football game on television. For some it means curling up with a good book and a box of chocolates. For others it means going to parties, or vacationing at the shore, or playing golf with their buddies on weekends.

I can remember, when I was a midshipman in the Navy, spending a weekend at a resort hotel on Lake Sunapee in New Hampshire. Wonderful food, lovely women, dancing, singing, strolling on the lake shore in the moonlight — it was a perfect weekend. I can recall that last dip in the lake, the cool, silvery water so fresh and invigorating on a hot Sunday afternoon in August. And I can remember saying to myself, "This is the life!"

Yes, the good life seems to be doing what one most enjoys. You don't hear people say, "This is the life!" when they are sitting in a dentist's chair having a root canal, or lying in a hospital bed after a hip replacement, or trading elbow jabs on a crowded subway, or changing a flat tire on a lonely road at night.

No, real living, it would seem, has to be fun, and for many people the spicier the better. A college sophomore told his roommate, "You should have been with me last night. I was really living!"

"What do you mean?" asked his friend.

"I was stoned man, stoned!"

To some people, real living means loose living, letting their hair down, feeling no inhibitions, having a wild time. For them living means living it up!

But that's not what it meant to the apostle Paul. "For to me living is Christ," he said. The goal of Paul's life, his reason for being, his motivating passion, his dominant desire was Jesus Christ.

Note the context of Paul's affirmation. He was a prisoner at Rome, writing to his Christian friends at Philippi a letter of encouragement and hope. He assured them that his imprisonment had really served to advance the gospel, for it became widely known that he was a prisoner for Christ, and most of the believers were emboldened by his example to speak the word of God without fear. Paul did not know what the future held in store for him, but he confidently expected that he would honor Christ, whether by life or by death.

"For to me, living is Christ, and dying is gain," he declared. "If I am to live in the flesh, that means fruitful labor for me; and I do not know which I prefer. I am hard pressed between the two: my desire is to depart and be with Christ, for that is far better, but to remain in the flesh is more necessary for you" (Philippians 1:21-24). For Paul the choice between life or death was obviously not an easy one. To live was to go on proclaiming the gospel of Christ. To die was to be with Christ.

Paul's words inspired this 19th century hymn by Henry Harbaugh:

> *Jesus, I live to thee, the loveliest and best;*
> > *my life in thee, thy life in me, in thy blest love I rest.*
> *Jesus, I die to thee, whenever death shall come.*
> > *To die in thee is life to me, in my eternal home.*
> *Whether to live or die, I know not which is best;*

to live in thee is bliss to me, to die is endless rest.
Living or dying, Lord, I ask by to be thine;
my life in thee, thy life in me, makes heaven forever
mine.

Thus for Paul to die was gain — not the act of dying but what it signified. It was to be with his risen Lord, to know in full what he now knew only in part, to enter into the heavenly kingdom where pain and sorrow shall be no more. For himself Paul may have preferred this alternative, but for the sake of his friends he knew that to remain in the flesh was better, for they needed him. The thought of his death must have upset them, so that Paul wrote these words of hope. For himself he would prefer to die and be with Christ, but as long as he lived in the flesh he would devote his life to serving Christ. To him living was Christ.

How different are the words of Paul from the familiar soliloquy of Hamlet, the melancholy prince of Denmark. "To be or not to be — that is the question,"[22] mused the young prince — a relevant question for one contemplating suicide. But not for Paul, and not for us. To *live* or not to *live*, *that* is the question for you and me, and unless we have discovered the joy of what Paul called "being in Christ," we'll never know what living really means.

Jesus came in order that we may have life, and have it abundantly (John 10:10). In Jesus Christ we are free to live. He said, "I am the resurrection and the life. Those who believe in me, even though they die, will live" (John 11:25). To be in Christ, then, is to have life. "This is the testimony," said John: "God gave us eternal life, and this life is in God's Son. Whoever has the Son has life; whoever does not have the Son of God does not have life" (I John 5:11-12). To John, as to Paul, living was Christ. The life John was writing about was eternal life, and it is offered to us as a gift. When we have this life, we can *really* live. We can have life and have it abundantly. "I write these things to you who believe in the name of the Son of God, so that you may know that you have eternal life" (I John 5:13) — that you *have* eternal life, present tense! Eternal life begins the moment you give your heart to Christ.

Being free to live in and for Christ, means being free to live for others, free to serve him by serving others. That's the freedom to which we are called but which many who call themselves Christians have never experienced. Why? Because they are not really living for Christ. That is, he is not their dominant desire, the goal of their living.

If it is true that everyone has some basic drive, some motivating principle around which his or her life is oriented, it is more likely to be a drive for material possessions, or social status, or political power. Many are motivated by a desire to be famous, or successful, or popular. Some seek security, or the satisfaction of their personal pleasures or passions, while others find meaning in attaching themselves to a cause, or an ideal. It could be any one or a combination of these drives.

When these basic needs are being satisfied, a person feels that life is worthwhile. But one's ultimate satisfaction is not to be found in these pursuits alone, however satisfying they may temporarily be. Living is not possessions. It is not just having things. It is not just squirreling up for retirement in order to be able to enjoy the good things of life in one's latter years. Will Rogers, the homespun philosopher, was once asked by a friend, "If you had only 48 hours to live, how would you spend them?"

"One at a time!" said the famous cowboy.

Living is not a future but a present activity; life must be lived in the present, one day at a time, one hour at a time. Jesus said, "Do not worry about tomorrow, for tomorrow will bring worries of its own. Today's trouble is enough for today" (Matthew 6:34). That does not mean we shouldn't plan or have goals in life. What it means is that we should not put off living today for fear of what might happen tomorrow.

> *Living for some future day?*
> *Always wishing time away?*
> *To miss the moment of today*
> *is such a costly price to pay!*[23]

To live is not living for sex. St. Augustine discovered that. In his *Confessions* he tells the sordid story of his life before his conversion. By Hollywood standards he was really living. But not until he committed his life to Christ did he discover the unmatchable joy of being free to live for Christ.

To live is not having power. Adolph Hitler's life proved that. He had a cause and gave his life to it, but history has marked him as another pompous peacock whose mission was doomed because it was evil. In *Mein Kampf* he said, "By defending myself against the Jews I am doing the Lord's work." What arrogance, what hypocrisy, what sheer evil, to claim divine sanction for his heinous mission!

To live is not being wealthy. When John D. Rockefeller was asked how much money it takes to satisfy someone, his oft-quoted reply was "Just a little more!" His wealth did not prevent Vanderbilt from leaping to his death out of a twelfth-story window.

To live is not being famous. Why else have the lives of so many famous people ended in tragedy? Ernest Hemingway was a famous writer, but he blew his brains out.

For a Christian "really living" is not any of these things. To live is Christ. It is, as the gospel song says, "living for Jesus a life that is true, striving to please him in all that you do."[24] When one has this relationship with Christ, life becomes meaningful in all its aspects. That's the abundant life. Some things which once were all-important no longer seem quite as important. A new set of values makes the old life seem shallow and even empty. One's work takes on new meaning, when it is dedicated to Christ. One's occupation becomes one's vocation.

I remember a conversation I had with a young minister at a pastor's retreat. He told me he had not given the ministry a thought until he happened to ask a college senior what he was going to do after graduation. "I'm going to be a Christian farmer," said his friend. "That was a new thought to me," said the pastor who was telling me the story. "It completely broke down the barrier I had built up around myself. I was so impressed that I decided then and there to give my heart to Christ and to let him direct my life from then on. And here I am."

Life is fuller in every respect, when one is living for Christ. Friendships are deeper, pleasures are purer, goals are nobler, ideals are higher, intentions are holier. There is also a greater appreciation of the little pleasures of life, things so often taken for granted. In Thornton Wilder's *Our Town*, young Emily dies, but she is allowed to go back to a scene from her childhood, where she relives the fleeting memories of long ago. With a new appreciation for the life she lived, she exclaims:

> *It goes so fast. We don't have time to look at one another ... I realize.... So all that was going on and we never noticed.... One more look.... Good-bye.... Good-bye, world.... Good-bye, Grovers Corners ... Mama and Papa.... Good-bye to clocks ticking ... and Mama's sunflowers.... And food and coffee.... And new-ironed dresses and hot baths ... and sleeping and waking up.... Oh, Earth, you're too wonderful for anybody to realize you. Do any human beings ever realize life, while they live it — every, every minute?*[25]

Yes, life is precious, and we are given only one life to live. "One life, a little gleam of time between two eternities; no second chance for us forevermore," commented Thomas Carlyle.[26] A middle-aged man must have discovered that truth in church one Sunday morning, for he commented to my wife after the service, "I'm an elder of the church and I can't begin to tell you how many committees I've been serving on. But I realized this morning for the first time that I've been faking it for twenty years. I have been living my life for me, not for Christ."

That kind of honest confession is the doorway to a new life in Christ. Now is always the right time to ask oneself, Have I really turned my life over to Christ? Can I truthfully say with Paul, "To me, living is Christ"? If you feel your life is meaningless and drab, confess that to God and tell God you sincerely want Christ to come into your life.

Do you really want to live in and for him? That's what it means to be a Christian. It's not enough to belong to a church; any hypocrite can do that. It's not enough to live a "good" life; an atheist can do that. It's not enough to believe in God; even the Devil does. Christianity is not a code of ethics, or a system of doctrine, or a creedal statement. Christianity is a *relationship* with Jesus Christ.

It is to identify with a person, not just a man who died, but a Savior who lives; not just a dead hero, but a living Lord, who is "the same yesterday, today, and forever" (Hebrews 13:8).

God in Christ offers every human being the freedom to live a life with meaning and hope and joy and confidence: a life of meaning, because it is a life of service; a life of hope, because we know the future is in God's hands; a life of joy, because, like the apostle Paul, we know the secret of Christian contentment; a life of confidence, because we know that "all things work for good with those who love God, those who are called according to his purpose" (Romans 8:28), and because we know that nothing can separate us from the love of God, which is in Christ Jesus our Lord (Romans 8:38-39).

For freedom Christ has set us free. So claim your freedom, and live!

Questions For Personal Reflection
And/Or Group Discussion

1. What is "the good life" for you? When do you feel most fulfilled and happy? What makes life worthwhile?

2. Paul said "living is Christ." He talked about being "in Christ." What do these expressions mean to you?

3. We hear much talk about "the right to life." Is life a right or a gift? Why do you feel the way you do about life?

4. Jesus came that we might have life and have it abundantly? What is that abundant life and have you experienced it? If so, when and how?

5. How would you explain the relationship between the Christian life and Christian freedom?

6. What is "eternal life" and what are its implications for everyday living?

Chapter Six

Who, Me?
Free To Witness

In the 4th Gospel John has recorded his version of Jesus' long discourse with his disciples at the Last Supper. One of the things Jesus said to them was that after he was gone, the Holy Spirit would be sent to bear witness to him, and, he said, "you also are witnesses, because you have been with me from the beginning" (John 15:27).

As a parting reminder, the last thing Jesus said to his disciples before his ascension, was that they should be his witnesses, in Jerusalem, and in all Judea, and Samaria and to the end of the earth (Acts 1:8). He has never rescinded that command. Those who believe in him, like the disciples of old and all his followers ever since, have been commissioned to be his faithful witnesses.

Every time I say something like that to a typical mainline congregation some people look as if they're sitting there thinking, "Who, me?" To which I want to reply, "Yes, you!" Every Christian is a witness for Christ. That's what the name Christian (*Christ*-ian) implies. Not everyone is gifted to be an evangelist, however that word is defined. But every Christian is a witness.

The question is not, Am I or am I not a witness? The question is, What kind of witness am I? If I call myself a Christian, I am a witness whether I like it or not, whether I deny it or not. The question is not, Am I willing to be a witness, but, What kind of witness am I willing to be?

The English word "witness" is used to translate the New Testament Greek word *martus*, from which comes the English word "martyr." A Christian martyr was a person who suffered death because of his or her faith in Jesus Christ. Countless numbers of believers have laid down their lives for Christ across the centuries

57

and even in our own time. Although most Christians will never have to suffer martyrdom, they are nevertheless called to be witnesses.

In a court of law witnesses are those who testify to something they have seen or heard, those who are called upon to give evidence about something they know. To be a Christian witness is to bear testimony to what one has seen, and heard, and knows, about Jesus Christ. It is to tell others about him; but I can't do that unless I myself know him. To be a Christian witness is to give evidence that one has been with Jesus. "You are witnesses," Jesus told his disciples, "because you have been with me...."

As is the way with language, we often make verbs out of nouns. So we talk about "witnessing," which for a Christian means telling someone about Christ. Witnesses always point to someone other than themselves. Christian witnesses tell what they know about Christ. They testify from their personal experience, and one can't do that if one hasn't been with Jesus.

Luke tells us that when the elders, the scribes, and the high priestly family "saw the boldness of Peter and John, and perceived that they were uneducated, common (ordinary) men, they wondered; and they recognized that they (Peter and John) had been with Jesus" (Acts 4:13). I wonder if people watching us can recognize that we have been with Jesus?

It hardly needs saying that we witness with our deeds as well as with our words, by what we do as well as by what we say. In fact, the most effective proof of our devotion is the kind of life we live, and the quality of our life is the measure of the integrity of our witness. But witnessing is more than just living a good life, as important as that is. Too many Christians have used that as an excuse for not telling others the good news.

"I don't have to talk about it," they say rather self-righteously; "I'll show people by the way I live." Oh, really? Isn't that a rather arrogant claim? How would someone know I'm a Christian simply because I think that I'm a moral person, that I'm compassionate, considerate, and kind? Non-Christians can be just as moral, just as compassionate, considerate, and kind.

Actions speak louder than words, it is true, but actions without words do not edify or explain. Actions without words do not disclose the reason for, nor reveal the power behind, nor point to the goal of their existence. Actions without words may easily attract attention to themselves, instead of pointing to the one who inspires them. Words without actions are the badge of hypocrisy, that's true; but actions without words may be the sign of timidity. Life-style without reference to Christ is not Christian witnessing. Sooner or later a word must be spoken, a faith must be communicated, the good news must be heard. People need to know who inspires and enables our good deeds.

So both are necessary, actions *and* words. No one argues about the former. But some folks squirm when anyone suggests that they need to talk about their faith as well as live it, that they have to talk the talk, as well as walk the walk. Who, me? Because of that too frequently held view, in this chapter I want to focus on how to witness with our words. Many Christians have never known the joy of telling someone else about Jesus. They've never even tried!

Why? Why are many church members so timid if not terrified about sharing their faith? Why are some so resentful if not angry at the suggestion that this is something a Christian ought to do? Is it because they don't want to, or is it because they don't know how to? Many objections have to do with people's phobia's — the fear of rejection, or of failure, or of offending someone, the fear of being considered a fanatic. They're afraid they don't know enough about the Bible, or about theology, or about Christianity, or whatever. They don't want to be like those characters who all but pound people over the head with a Bible ("The Bible says...!"), or who attack you verbally ("Repent, you sinner!"), or who threaten you with the dire consequences of your not accepting *their* version of the gospel ("If you haven't had a born again experience, you are not a Christian and you'll end up in hell!"

Nor do the reluctant witnesses want to invade people's privacy; "After all, faith is a personal thing," they argue. "You shouldn't talk about religion; it's not polite. It's un-American!"

But Jesus said, Be my witnesses! Who, me? Not me! That's for those crazy Pentecostals, and rabid fundamentalists, and over-zealous evangelicals, not for sophisticated, well-bred, well-educated, well-healed main-liners like us! Oh? Is that what Jesus had in mind? He didn't say, "You evangelicals and fundamentalists shall be my witnesses, but not you Methodists, or you Presbyterians, or you Episcopalians, or you Lutherans."

And he didn't say, "I want you theologians to be my witnesses but not you pastors, or I want you pastors to be my witnesses but not you lay people." He said "You (that's everyone who claims to be his disciple) shall be my witnesses!" Bearing witness to Jesus Christ is a discipline that can be practiced by anyone, anywhere, any time. You don't have to go to seminary to learn how. You don't have to have "Rev." in front of your name to entitle you to do it. You don't have to be a professional speaker. The freedom to which we are called in Christ includes the freedom to witness.

Witnessing is not a theological debate. It's not a sales pitch. It's not an academic discussion. It's certainly not an argument to be won. Witnessing is simply a matter of sharing your own faith, in your own words, in your own way. You don't have to prove how much you know about the Bible, or what a great Christian you are. That can be intimidating to other people, if not offensive. You just relate your own faith experience. You talk about the God you know personally, about the Christ who is real to you, about the church you love. You can do that with confidence, because everyone is an authority on one's own experience. What has God done for you lately? That's what you talk about.

But when and how do you do that? There are right ways and wrong ways to witness for Christ. I believe every Christian, deep down in his or her heart, would like to be a better witness for Christ. Here are some of the basic principles which I try to remember in my own interpersonal witnessing. The first thing I try to remember is that I must BE PREPARED. By that I mean being aware of as well as ready for opportunities to witness. Most of us have all kinds of opportunities, but too often we let them slip by. There must be a conscious desire on our part to accept every opportunity God gives us to witness. For instance, someone may ask you why you aren't laughing at their foul jokes, or why you do or don't do this or that, or why you feel the way you do about something. That's your chance. Even if you only say something like this: "I'm just trying to do what I believe in my heart Christ wants me to do." That's witnessing. There's much more to be said, of course, but that's a start.

It's consistent with what the apostle Peter meant when he said, "Always be ready to give an answer to anyone who asks you for a reason for the hope that is within you" (I Peter 3:15a). You can usually tell when someone with whom you are talking is searching for answers, trying to find some meaning in the midst of the hectic demands and frantic pace of life, some hope in time of trouble, sickness, or sorrow. Be ready to share your experience of God, the God who has revealed such great love for us in Jesus Christ.

Being prepared means being ready for as well as being aware of opportunities for witnessing. We need to do some thinking about what we believe and why we believe it. That's what faith-sharing training programs like the *Faithful Witnesses* course[27] are designed to help people do. They help church members to understand their own faith and to feel comfortable talking about it. The participants learn from one another, and they reinforce each other's faith in the process, as together they study and practice how to draw upon the wisdom, power, and inspiration of the Bible in their witnessing.

Being an effective witness for Christ involves the desire and the commitment to learn what one needs to know. How can a Christian not be interested? It boils down to this: Do I believe in Jesus Christ or not? Will I obey him or not? He said "Be my witnesses!" What am I doing to equip myself for that responsibility?

To be a disciple is to be a learner. That's what the word means. Anyone who is really serious about wanting to be a better witness will take advantage of every opportunity to learn whatever one needs to learn to be a more effective witness, a more faithful steward, a more loyal disciple — in short, a better Christian.

The truth is, I can't call myself a Christian and say I don't care about becoming a better witness. That's a built-in contradiction! To be a *faithful* witness is to be one who is always striving to be a *better* witness.

One of the most important things one learns in the process is that a witness must BE SENSITIVE. That's the second principle I try to remember and follow. Always be ready to give a reason for the hope that is within you, "yet do it with gentleness and reverence" (I Peter 3:15b). Too often people leave out the second part of that text, when they use it as a proof text for witnessing. Share your faith, but do it with sensitivity. Christ wouldn't want his witnesses to cram their faith down other people's throats. That wasn't Jesus' style. He doesn't want us to force ourselves on others; he never did. A Christian witness should be tactful and gracious, never pushy or rude. If we embarrass or offend people by being overly aggressive, the effectiveness of our witness will be lost. We want to attract people to Christ, not drive them away. We don't win people by being judgmental, or self-righteous, or antagonistic. We can't argue people into the kingdom. We may win the argument, but we'll lose the person. A faithful witness is sensitive to other people's feelings.

That means we have to listen, and that's the third rule I want always to remember: BE A LISTENER. Though the freedom to which we are called includes the freedom to speak, I believe a witness must earn the right to be heard. We have to listen before we speak. Most people think learning to witness means learning only what to say. Not so. The most important skill in witnessing is listening. Good witnesses are always good listeners. We win the right to be heard by listening sensitively and caringly to the other person. That means listening with our heart as well as with our ears. It's listening not just to the words that are said, but to the feelings behind the words. We have to listen to know where the other person is "coming from," so that we can plug into the other person's experience.

When we do speak, we make it personal. That's the fourth principle I try to remember: BE PERSONAL! We don't have to pretend to have all the answers. We don't have to come up with a biblical proof text for every situation we encounter. We certainly don't want to give a theological dissertation. Faith sharing is heart-to-heart not head-to-head talk, personal not theoretical. In Christ we are free to share our own faith experience, as it relates to the other person's need.

62

So, to someone burdened by guilt, we can talk about the God who has forgiven us in Jesus Christ. To someone anxious about the future, we can share how God has provided for us. To someone desperate for answers, we can talk about our own answered prayers and how the Holy Spirit has guided us when we've put our trust in God. People may argue with a theory, or with your opinion about something, but they can't deny you your experience and what it means to you. So be personal!

Understand, that does not mean forcing one's experience on someone else. You don't offer your experience as proof of the existence of God. You're simply telling the other person why you believe. You can't talk about a God you don't know personally. You can't bear witness to a Savior you've never met. Our task as witnesses is not to try to prove that Jesus is the Christ. That we can never do. Our role as witnesses is to show by the way we speak and act that we believe he is. That by God's grace we can do!

That leads to my fifth principle for witnessing: BE PRAYER-FUL. God is the ultimate and the only converter of human hearts. It is not our words that save but the Holy Spirit speaking through us. You and I are only witnesses to what *God* has done and can do. We plant seeds. We water seeds that others have planted. But it is God who gives the growth (I Corinthians 3:6). If our effectiveness as witnesses depended upon our own eloquence or cleverness of speech, or upon our own ability to say just the right words at the right time, then we would have cause to worry about witnessing.

Fortunately for us as well as for those to whom we witness, that is not the case. Jesus told his disciples not to be anxious beforehand about what they should say when they were on trial for their faith, "for what you are to say will be given to you in that hour; for it is not you who speak, but the Spirit of your Father speaking through you" (Mt. 10:19-20). Every faithful witness has experienced the truth of those words. It's not you and I, but the Holy Spirit speaking through us. What a freeing thought that is! The Holy Spirit frees us to witness! We work as if it all depends on us, but we pray knowing that it all depends on God. Our task is to be faith-full — full of faith, knowing that God can use our humblest efforts to work miracles in people's lives, not because of any virtue in us, but because of God's marvelous grace and love, not *because* of us but *in spite of* us. If we pray for God's help and rely on Jesus' promise, God will put the words in our mouth. Even if we stammer and stutter and fumble for words, God's purpose will be accomplished, if we are sincere. What a tremendous burden that lifts from our shoulders! For freedom Christ has set us free to witness!

There is much more to be said about interpersonal witnessing and faith sharing. The principles I have identified in this chapter are important but by no means exhaustive. Of the many other things that could yet be mentioned, I want to identify just one more rule which those who take seriously their responsibility to be Christ's witnesses need to remember: BE PERSISTENT! Leaving the result of a faith-sharing conversation to God does not mean forgetting about it. We don't abandon our own responsibility by turning it over to God. On the contrary, we have to keep on turning it over. That means we have to be persistent in our concern for others, persistent in our availability, persistent in prayer. Many churches as well as individual witnesses have not been persistent enough to discover that persistence pays off! To be Christ's witness implies a commitment to be available to those we seek to reach in the name of Christ. It is to be what we are called to be: the servant people of God, following in the footsteps of one who came as a suffering servant, and who bids his followers deny themselves, and take up a cross, and follow him!

That's why the church is so important, for we witness as members of a community of faith, the body of Christ, a caring family of believers who are committed to ministering to people's needs both within and beyond the walls of the church.

What an encouragement, what a comfort, what a joy, to know that we are not alone in this enterprise! That's why we want to bring people into the church, where they can get the help we can't give them by ourselves, where they can learn what others can teach them, where they can be spiritually and intellectually nourished in and by the whole community of faith, and where they can take their place as fellow witnesses and disciples of Christ.

Jesus Christ has commissioned those who bear his name to be his witnesses wherever they may be in this world, this world that so desperately needs to hear the good news that has been entrusted to all of us who believe in him. Will we accept the commission? Will we answer the call? If we won't, who will? If we can't, who can?

Imagine yourself having this conversation with Jesus, when he says to you:

Be my witness![28]

Who, me?	*Yes, you!*
Not me!	*You, too!*
Who says?	*I do!*
Why me?	*You'll do.*
Who else?	*Too few.*
It's hard!	*What's new?*
I'll goof.	*That's true.*
Can I?	*Not you.*
Then how?	*We two!*
I see!	*You do?*
I do	*Then do!*

Questions For Personal Reflection And/Or Group Discussion

1. When has God seemed most real to you? Under what circumstances do you feel closest to God?

2. Who was most influential in your Christian faith development? Has anyone ever "witnessed" to you? What was your reaction?

3. What do you understand your role to be as a witness for Jesus Christ? How would you rate yourself as a witness?

4. What are your concerns about witnessing? Are there barriers that keep you from being the kind of witness your Christian conscience is prodding you to be?

5. What are you doing to help yourself become a more faithful and effective witness? Is your church helping you?

6. Have you ever passed up an opportunity to witness to someone? Can you think of some unchurched person with whom you could have a faith-sharing conversation?

Chapter Seven

Tell Me About It!
Free To Listen

In a file of cartoons I've collected over the years there's an old "Grin and Bear It" illustration showing two women in the waiting room of a doctor's office. One is saying to the other, "It's agreed, Adele! We'll trade symptoms and find out if he really listens."

In the preceding chapter the point was made that to be an effective witness one must first be a good listener. A Turkish proverb declares, "If speech is silver, listening is gold." There always has been and there always will be a need for good listeners. Taylor Caldwell made this point quite poignantly years ago in her popular book, *The Listener*. As I was thinking about this topic, I reread parts of it. Caldwell tells about a wise old man named John Godfrey, who shortly before his death established a beautiful sanctuary to which people could come to tell their troubles in private to someone who would always be there to listen.

"What do you expect people to say in here?" asked a reporter, when the sanctuary was first opened. "They will know before they come," Godfrey replied. "One of the most terrible aspects of this world today is that nobody listens to anyone else. If you are sick, or even dying, nobody listens. If you are bewildered, or frightened, or lost, or bereaved, or alone, or lonely —nobody really listens."

So great is people's need to be heard that they are willing to pay psychoanalysts, therapists, pastoral counselors, and other professionals just to listen to them. Why don't most of us listen more than we do? I'm referring to people with normal hearing. Deaf people listen better with their eyes than most of us do with our ears. They concentrate. They pay attention. They want to be sure they understand what's being said. Lack of hearing ability is not the reason most of us don't listen.

Why, then, do we not listen better than we do? For one thing, we're too busy. We have no time for listening, or at least we think we don't. We have too many things we've got to get done, too many demands on our time, too much on our mind. Even when we do listen, we do it only half-heartedly. We're too preoccupied with our own thoughts, our own needs, our own problems and concerns to listen to anyone else. "Tell me about it!" we say, which really means "If you think *you've* got troubles, mine are just as bad if not worse!"

Not only are we too busy and too preoccupied, many of us don't really know how to listen. Archie Bunker put it this way: "The reason you don't understand me, Edith, is because I'm talking to you in English and you're listening in dingbat!" In recognition of the fact that people don't know how to listen, there has been a proliferation of books about listening. Experts in communication theory have developed a whole new vocabulary and their erstwhile jargon words have become familiar terms to many people. Despite the plethora of workshops, seminars, and courses designed to teach listening skills, most people still don't know how to listen. It is ironic that although most communication between human beings has always been oral, public and private schools alike have traditionally spent much time teaching children to read and write and practically no time teaching them to listen.

Recognizing that omission, some schools are now giving their students formal training in listening. Many colleges and universities are also providing courses in listening, and some churches have formed listening groups to give people the opportunity to listen and to be heard.

There are web sites offering to "listen" to people's problems. "No one to talk to?" asked one I came across recently. "Talk to someone who cares! Call NEO TEENLINE." The web page included this disclaimer: "We are a listening service. We do not tell callers what to do, but help callers identify their own problems."

Another web site lists what hundreds of famous and not-so-famous persons have said about listening. "The best way to persuade people is with your ears — by listening to them," declares one contributor, former Secretary of State Dean Rusk. And television anchor-woman and news commentator Diane Sawyer, is quoted as saying "I think the one lesson I have learned is that there is no substitute for paying attention."

No substitute indeed, but those who teach listening skills have to deal with the fact that we human beings think faster than we can talk. While the average American speaks at the rate of about 125 words a minute, ideas race through a normal person's brain at much higher speeds. The more than 13 billion cells in the human brain operate with amazing speed and efficiency.

Thus our brains can receive spoken words and still have spare time for thinking. Studies of the listening abilities of thousands of students and business and professional people have revealed that most people do not use their spare thinking time wisely, as they listen. Most of us tend to go on mental side-tracks, and in doing so we miss part of what the speaker is saying. We also tend to memorize facts, instead of listening for ideas, and this, too, impedes our ability to listen.

Still another detriment to good listening is our tendency to employ emotional filters in the hearing process. We listen attentively to what we want to hear, while shutting out what we don't want to hear. Too often our critical faculties are crippled by our emotional involvement. When someone hits upon one of our pet peeves or prejudices, we stop listening and begin mentally rehearsing all of our objections. Every preacher is familiar with this tendency!

There's another reality that those who teach listening skills need to acknowledge. Being a good listener involves more than listening skills. We can know *how* to listen, but if we don't want to listen, we won't listen well. Human beings can teach listening skills, but only God can make a good listener. Listening is liking giving. Nothing happens to a persons' giving until something happens to the person, and nothing happens to a person's listening until something happens to the person. Good listening involves a change of heart, and that's God's work. Listening skills, such as knowing how to paraphrase, how to do perception checks, and how to do behavior descriptions, can be learned, but compassion and the commitment to help another person are gifts of God. Only God can make us compassionate and generous and caring.

It is not unfair to say, therefore, that listening is *not* one of humankind's most notable attributes. And yet, God wants us to listen. God has given us this delicate instrument called an ear, a highly sensitive and intricately specialized organ, which for people with normal hearing is capable of functioning over an energy range of nearly two trillion times. It is said that in the middle frequencies, where sounds vibrate from about 1000 to 4000 cycles per second, human beings have developed the maximum sensitivity it is practical to possess, for if the ears were any keener, they would respond unbearably to the unceasing molecular motions of the air particles.

Whether or not we have been blessed with the ability to hear, we have the capacity to listen. But how we waste it! We don't listen as well as we could and should to others, and we don't listen as well as we could and should to God. When I don't listen to others, I fail myself and I fail others. I fail myself, because when I don't listen, I don't learn. I fail *them*, because when I don't listen; I don't understand; and when I don't understand, I can't help them. How many tragic mistakes could have been avoided if someone had only listened? How many teenage suicides, how many high school shootings, how many hate crimes, how many vengeful deeds, how many acts of violence, how many misunderstandings could be prevented, if people would only listen? And how many more souls might be won to Christ, if more well-meaning witnesses would learn to listen before they speak?

When I don't listen, I also fail God, for the freedom to which God calls us in Jesus Christ includes the freedom to listen to one another and to God. When I'm too busy to listen, too preoccupied with my own concerns to listen to God or to a fellow human being, I am neglecting a most precious freedom. God wants us to listen to one another, and God wants us to listen to *God*. "O that my people would listen to me!" (Psalm 81:13). The Old Testament prophets cried out in despair at Israel's refusal to listen to the word of God. "For twenty-three years ... the word of the LORD has come to me," moaned Jeremiah, "and I have spoken persistently to you, but you have not listened" (Jeremiah 25:3). "O that you had hearkened to my commandment!" spoke Isaiah in the name of the LORD (Isaiah 48:18).

70

And in the New Testament we hear Jesus utter this terse command: "Let anyone with ears listen!" (Matthew 11:15, 13:9, Mark 4:9, *etc.*). On the Mount of Transfiguration, the voice of God declares, "This is my beloved Son, with whom I am well pleased; listen to him!" (Matthew 17:5).

Listening to God is not just an obligation on our part. It is a tremendous privilege. It's a right that we should cherish and never fail to use. God wants us to listen for at least three reasons: first, when we listen, God can help us. "O that my people would listen to me ... I would soon subdue their enemies and turn my hand against their foes" (Psalm 81:14). Applying that promise to our own lives, I take it to mean that if we listen to God, God will help us to subdue *our* enemies: fear, worry, sorrow, bitterness, envy, self-pity, pride, guilt.

To John Godfrey's sanctuary came men and women with all kinds of problems and needs. As they talked to the unseen Listener, they felt their burdens lifted and their hearts strengthened. Though he never spoke, they felt as if they could hear him, and soon they found themselves listening for his response. One by one they came and found their needs met, when they talked to the Listener hidden behind a thick blue curtain. On the wall beside the curtain was a brass plate that said, "If you wish to see the one who has listened to you, touch the button above." Behind the curtain was a painting of the face of Jesus.

If we listen, God will help us. Second, God will also teach us. "O that Israel would walk in my ways!" (Psalm 81:13). Only as we tune our hearts to the voice of the Holy Spirit, can we know the way God would have us walk. Not only did those who talked to the Listener find relief from their cares. They also found understanding and were given new insight and clarity that they had not known before. With their new understanding came a new sense of direction and purpose for their lives.

If we listen, God will teach us, God will help us, and third, God will forgive us. The assurance of God's love and forgiveness can come in no other way than through the listening heart of the believer, a heart that is receptive to the gospel of Christ. If we don't listen to that message, how can we know the reality of God's forgiveness?

Granted these important reasons for listening to God, how does one do that? How does one listen to God? Through prayer, of course, and meditation, and worship, and devotional reading of the Scriptures. The essential point is that God will speak to anyone who really listens. When we pray as listeners, we will understand how God answers our prayers. That means praying humbly and submissively, in the manner of our Lord, who prayed, "Nevertheless not my will, but thine, be done" (Luke 22:42; cf. Matthew 26:39). God may speak to us through other persons, or events, or circumstances, or simply in the silence of one's own thoughts, in any number of ways. In order to hear God's voice, however, we must ever be seeking to discern and to do God's will; that is, listening for what God wants to say to us.

The obvious implication of the previous paragraph is that listening to God is not just a function of the ears. Right listening must also involve one's mind, and heart, and will. It is interesting that in the ancient Hebrew language there was no specific word corresponding to our English verb "to obey." The translators used the word "obey" to bring out the full meaning of the Hebrew verb "to hear." Thus to listen to God means to respond in obedience to God's will. "Blessed are those who hear the word of God and keep it," said Jesus (Luke 11:28).

In Jesus Christ we are called to freedom, and that includes the freedom to listen. By the grace of Christ we can be freed of the egotism, the selfishness and self-centeredness, the preoccupation with our own affairs, and everything else that keeps us from listening to God and to one another. To be one in Christ is to be one with each other. Jesus helps us reorder our priorities so that we are not too busy to listen to God or to a neighbor in need. Indeed, when we do listen to a neighbor in need, with compassion, empathy, and commitment, we have listened to Christ, who said "as you did it to one of the least of these, my brothers or sisters, you did it to me" (Matthew 25:40).

When we learn to listen as God in Christ frees us to listen, we discover the wonderful truth that God himself is the never-failing Listener. This is what those who went to John Godfrey's sanctuary discovered. What a comfort to know that in this hectic world of interstate highways and supersonic jets, cell phones and laptop computers, fluctuating stock markets and political posturing, television and telemarketing, and countless other distractions, we have a Savior who is never too busy to listen, who is always available, who knows us better than we know ourselves, and who can help us in any and all circumstances, when we sincerely seek his will.

And what a comfort it is to realize that we can do that, because in freedom Christ has set us free — to listen! I offer this prayer for those who want to become better listeners:

> *Teach me to listen, Lord. Help me discern*
> *your divine will for my life. Let me learn*
> *how to give heed to your voice, when you speak,*
> *that in all choices your truth I may seek.*
> *Teach me to listen, Lord, that I might see*
> *always you faithfully listen to me.*
> *Teach me to listen, Lord, that I may grow*
> *with each new insight you want me to know.*
> *Teach me to listen, Lord, that I may find*
> *how to attend you with heart, soul, and mind.*
> *Make me compassionate, willing to give.*
> *Teach me to listen, Lord, that I may live.*[29]

Questions For Personal Reflection And/Or Group Discussion

1. On a scale if 0 (not at all) to 10 (excellent) how would you rate yourself as a listener? What is the reason for your self-rating? Do others consider you a good listener?

2. Do you think you would have listened better to Jesus than the Twelve did?

3. Most of us listen better sometimes than we do at other times. When do you listen best? What keeps you from being a better listener?

4. The point is made in this chapter that listening to others and to God is not just an obligation but a tremendous privilege. How does Christ free us to listen?

5. When do you listen best to God? How do you know you are listening to God? Do you listen when you pray?

6. Do you ever meditate? When, and how, and with what results?

Chapter Eight

Sorry Is Not Enough
Free To Confess

We have heard it said that confession is good for the soul. Then why don't we do it more often? Roman Catholics are supposed to confess their sins to a priest at least once a year. It is part of the sacrament of penance, which includes repenting of one's sins, confessing them to a priest, accepting some act of devotion or discipline as a proof of one's penitence (Catholics call it "doing penance"), and being absolved of one's sins by the priest.

The corporate prayer of confession which is said in many churches during the Sunday morning worship service, followed by the assurance of pardon, is the Protestant liturgical substitute for the sacrament of penance, but I doubt if it has the same therapeutic or psychological value as the sacrament has for Catholics.

Not surprisingly, there are some Protestants who resent having to say the corporate prayer of confession in worship. A man accosted me after worship one Sunday morning to complain about that part of the service. "If I'm not guilty, why should I have to confess?" he asked defiantly. "And if I *am* guilty, that's between me and God!" The corporate prayer of confession is meaningful for those who take it seriously, but obviously it is not specific enough, especially if it is one of the familiar, generic prayers so often used, which do not usually involve any serious soul-searching and acknowledging of an individual's specific foibles, faults, and failures. That is why many Protestant churches include in their liturgy, right before or after the corporate prayer, a time for silent confession of personal sins.

There is certainly some purpose and value in asking for God to pardon our sins in general, but we also need to confess our particular sins not only to God but to each other, as James, the brother of our Lord, instructed: "Therefore confess your sins to one another..." (James 5:16a). James did not say whether this should be done publicly or privately, nor did he say it should be done to a priest. What James said does not refute that practice, nor does it sanction it. There was no Christian priesthood, of course, when James wrote his letter.

Until the end of the fourth century A.D. the practice was for penitent Christians to confess their sins publicly. This led to difficulties, however, as penitent sinners were often not permitted to forget their mistakes. Their antagonists in the church would use their confession to harass, annoy, and even to prosecute confessed sinners.

It is not difficult to understand how this could happen, human nature being what it is. The danger is amusingly illustrated in the classic story, which ministers love to tell, about a group of pastors who decided it would be good for them to get together privately and confess their secret sins to one another. When they met the following week, the Baptist pastor was the first to volunteer: "My weakness is alcohol. I confess that I drink too much, yet I tell my people they should not drink"

"My big sin is gambling," said the Methodist minister. "I enjoy sneaking off to the race track every chance I get." One by one the pastors unburdened themselves, confiding their deep, dark secrets. Finally, the Presbyterian minister stood up. "Well, friends, this has been most interesting, but I must be going now."

"But you haven't confessed your sin yet," said the others.

"Oh, yes," came the quick reply. "My sin is that I'm an uncontrollable gossip. Good day, brothers and sisters!" Needless to say, the pastors were not eager to repeat their experiment in public confession!

Because of problems like this, over a period of time it became the practice to assign to certain priests the duty of holding preliminary hearings to decide whether or not the penitent sinner should confess to the congregation. Since even this precaution did not prevent the gossips and critics from misusing what they heard, the practice of public confession was eventually replaced by private confession.

In A.D. 459 Pope Leo the First dealt a severe blow to public penance by officially sanctioning private confession. The admission of one's sins and the fixing of penance by the priest were the significant aspects of this practice for a long time, but this gradually changed, until absolution (the absolving of one's sins by the priest) became in actuality the most important element. Finally, at the 4th Lateran Council in A.D. 1215, the Roman Catholic Church made it obligatory for all Catholics who had reached the age of discretion to confess their sins at least once a year.

In view of such a long and gradual development it is interesting to read this canon from the Council of Trent in the mid-sixteenth century: "If anyone denies that sacramental confession was instituted by divine law, or is necessary for salvation, or says that the manner of confession secretly to a priest alone, *which the Catholic Church has always observed from the beginning* [italics mine], and still observes, is at variance with the institutions and command of Christ, and is a human invention, let him [sic.] be anathema."[30]

The Roman Catholic doctrine was totally unacceptable to the Protestant Reformer John Calvin, who bombastically declared: "Let all the hired ravers of the Pope babble as they may, we hold that Christ is not the author of this law, which compels men [sic.] to enumerate their sins; nay, that 1200 years elapsed after the resurrection of Christ before any such law was made."[31]

What, then, should we say about this matter of confession? A brief word study might be helpful here. The literal meaning of the Hebrew verb *yadah* was "to throw out the hand" or "to show by extending the hand," as one might do in giving thanks or praise. Indeed, of the 111 times that Hebrew verb is used in the Old Testament, in the English versions it is translated 93 times, "to praise" or "to give thanks," and only eighteen times "to confess" or "to make confession."

The two corresponding Greek verbs in the New Testament (*exomologeo* and *homologeo*) are translated to "confess," "profess," "acknowledge," or "declare." They are used only five times with the word sins. The Gospels of Matthew and Mark speak of the people who were baptized by John in the river Jordan, confessing their sins (Matthew 3:6, Mark 1:5). In the book of Acts we are told that converts came to Paul confessing and divulging their practices (19:18). James, as has already been mentioned, exhorted the brothers and sisters to confess their sins to one another, and John in his first letter testified that God will forgive us if we confess our sins (I John 1:9). In each of these cases the sense of the word is to acknowledge or admit one's faults, but it also implies the intention to correct one's sinful ways.

Elsewhere in the New Testament the word conveys the idea of declaring or acknowledging that something is so, as in professing or confessing one's belief in Christ: "God abides in those who confess that Jesus is the Son of God," wrote John, "and they abide in God" (I John 4:15). And Paul declared, "If you confess with your lips that Jesus is Lord and believe in your heart that God raised him from the dead, you will be saved" (Romans 10:9).

Thus we're dealing with a word that is rich in meaning, but my specific interest in this chapter is with its use in connection with the admission of sins. It is quite obvious that the Bible imposes upon us an obligation to confess our sins. The very command to repent and be baptized implies the need to confess, for how can there be repentance without confession?

While it is clearly our duty to confess our sins, it is also a *privilege*, for John also declared, "If we confess our sins, he who is faithful and just will forgive us our sins and cleanse us from all unrighteousness" (I John 1:9). What a tremendous promise! What a tremendous privilege for those who are called to freedom in Jesus Christ! When we neglect our duty to confess, we deny ourselves the benefits of confessing. The Bible testifies to the truth that God is faithful to God's promises, and that God is merciful to those who confess their sins. "No one who conceals transgressions will prosper, but one who confesses and forsakes them will obtain mercy," says the Old Testament proverb (Proverbs 28:13).

"Then I acknowledged my sin to you," wrote the Psalmist, "and I did not hide my iniquity; I said, 'I will confess my transgressions to the LORD,' and you forgave the guilt of my sin" (Psalms 32:5-6). In the 26th chapter of Leviticus we read how God, after threatening all manner of punishment if Israel did not obey his commandments, then promises to remember his covenant with them, "if they confess their iniquity and the iniquity of their ancestors" (26:40).

According to the Bible, then, God's forgiveness is contingent upon our confession. It is offered to all, but if we do not avail ourselves of God's invitation to confess, we can't receive God's forgiveness. God forgives the penitent, and that's a promise.

But that's not all. John mentioned another benefit to be derived from confessing our sins. "God will cleanse us from all unrighteousness." It's not that we won't sin any more, for as John put it rather bluntly, "If we say we have no sin, we deceive ourselves, and the truth is not in us" (I John 1:8). But when we confess our sins, God wipes the blackboard clean, so that we don't have to live with the guilt of our mistakes always staring us in the face.

Anyone who has truly acknowledged and honestly confessed her or his sins knows the feeling of relief it brings. I'm not talking about those vague admissions of our unworthiness which we express from time to time, usually well qualified: "I know I'm not perfect, Lord, but...." Nor am I referring to our corporate prayers of confession. I'm talking about our personal, specific sins. The longer we keep them to ourselves, the heavier the burden becomes. So why not confess our sins to a merciful God? That's really not too hard to do, since God won't tell anybody! Our secrets are safe with God, but would I be willing to let someone else say to me what I have admitted to God about myself? That's the real test of a humble spirit.

> *There are blotches on my character*
> *that everybody sees.*
> *I have obvious shortcomings,*
> *but my problem isn't these.*
> *No, my problem is my secret sins*
> *about which no one knows.*
> *I say no one, but I know that God*
> *is well aware of those.*
> *When I'm criticized unfairly and*
> *I start to moan and groan,*
> *I just wonder what they'd say if*
> *all my secret sins were known....*[31]

The question is, therefore, have I really confessed to God, if I haven't confessed to another person? Maybe that's why James exhorts us to confess our sins to one another. But it should be done in the context of prayer. "Confess your sins to one another, and pray for one another, so that you may be healed," James went on to say (James 5:16). The healing we pray for is spiritual as well as physical. For spiritual healing to take place, confession must be followed by forgiveness. By confessing our mistakes, we appease those we have injured or offended by our trespasses. Reasonable people don't stay angry with someone who has sincerely and humbly apologized to them. Furthermore, by sharing our shortcomings and weaknesses with each other within the community of faith we obtain mutual sympathy and counsel, and we are able to strengthen one another with our prayers.

But this is risky. Not everyone can handle another person's sins. One becomes very vulnerable when one admits one's weaknesses and exposes oneself to the kinds of criticism which such honesty and humility invite. There are virtues, therefore, in the Roman Catholic practice of confession, for the penitent person knows that the priest to whom he or she is confessing will not misuse the information.

John Calvin, while admitting that pastors are especially qualified to hear confessions, emphasized that it must be completely voluntary on the part of the penitent sinner, free of all tyranny and compulsion.[33] The power to absolve sin, moreover, belongs not to the minister or priest, but to God.

In their aversion to the confessional booth some Protestants have thrown the baby out with the bath water. They say they don't believe in private confession, so they never confess their sins privately *or* publicly. Church members who won't confess their sins to anyone else should at least be willing to talk with their pastor. And pastors need to make themselves more available to their members for that purpose. I'm not talking about psychological therapy here. People with psychological or serious emotional problems need to seek professional help. But pastors have something unique to offer normal people, who need to know about a Savior who died for our sins.

If we were perfectly honest, however, most of us would have to confess that confession doesn't come easily! There are many reasons for our reluctance to confess: self-righteousness, pride, self-consciousness, ignorance, apathy, prejudice. Unbelievers, of course, feel no obligation to confess to a God they don't believe in. Some people who call themselves believers don't confess to God because their self-righteousness blinds them to their sins. They don't confess to their fellow human beings because they are too worried about what others will think of them. So they put up a false front and hide behind a convenient facade, afraid to let anyone peek inside to see who they really are.

Some people go around for years with something on their conscience, lacking the courage to confess it. As a result, they become nervous, tense, insecure, guilt-ridden in the presence of the person they offended. How much happier they would be if only they would unburden themselves to someone. The best place to start is with God, who in Jesus Christ has liberated us from our fear of confessing to others.

Whenever I ask God's forgiveness for something I have done, God's answer comes back loud and clear: "Saying you're sorry is not enough!" I have to show it by the way I act. Jesus taught us that penitence must always be translated into action. That means correcting the wrongs we've done, apologizing to the person we've hurt, slandered, maligned, criticized unfairly, or treated unjustly. We must make amends wherever we can, and that includes confessing to the person to whom we may have said something untrue or unkind about someone else. It means owning up even to the mean thoughts we have been harboring toward another person.

How can we expect God to forgive us, if we are unwilling to ask forgiveness of each other? The Lord's prayer is our constant reminder that forgiving is not enough: we must also recognize our need *to be forgiven*. Now we can see why the Hebrew word for confession also meant praise and thanksgiving. The ideas are closely related, for out of the experience of confessing one's sins, comes the knowledge of God's forgiveness, which in turn brings forth a response of praise and thanksgiving and a desire to walk in God's ways. Confession makes possible the joy of reconciliation, and the good, clean feeling that comes with being at peace with oneself, with others, and with God.

I am not suggesting that churches return to the practice of public confession of private sins. Corporate prayers of confession are intended to be, and they can and should be, an adequate substitute for the practice of public confession in the early church. But they are no substitute for confessing our individual sins to God and to each other, especially to those whom we may have offended.

We who call ourselves Christians should have no hang-ups about acknowledging our sins, because we have the assurance of God's pardon when we do so honestly and sincerely. That's the good news we proclaim week after week in church following the prayer of confession. Let us rejoice, therefore, that we are free to confess, because, as we proclaim in the assurance of pardon every Sunday morning, in Jesus Christ we are forgiven!

> *... Then I'm thankful for God's mercy,*
> *and true penitence begins,*
> *when I realize God loves me*
> *— yes, despite my secret sins!*[34]

Questions For Personal Reflection
And/Or Group Discussion

1. How hard is it for you to confess your faults and failures to others? How hard is it to confess your sins honestly to God? Why is it hard or not hard for you?

2. What is the relation between confessing to others and confessing to God?

3. How do you feel about the corporate prayer of confession in public worship?

4. Do you agree that confessing one's sins is a privilege as well as a responsibility? Why?

5. Do you feel you are forgiven when you confess your sins? Why do you feel the way you do about it? How does Jesus Christ fit into your understanding of confession?

6. How would you explain the relationship between confession and Christian freedom?

Chapter Nine

Ours For The Asking
Free To Pray

What was the secret of Jesus' power? It was not just his words, for most of what he said had already been said by others. Of the 111 verses that compose the Sermon on the Mount, only eighteen of them cannot be found in earlier rabbinical writings. Nor was it his works, for Jesus himself bade his followers to look beyond his miracles. Nor was it the manner of his death, for others had also died by crucifixion.

It was not his words but the fact the *he* said them. It was not his miracles but the fact that *he* worked them. It was not his death, but the fact that it was *he* who died. And the secret of his power was his oneness with God. It was this unity with God that gave power to his words, power to his works, saving power to his death. Jesus' life was a life of prayer.

His disciples sensed this. "Lord, teach us to pray," they pleaded (Luke 11:1). "Lord, show us the Father and we shall be satisfied," said Philip (John 14:8). Jesus did show them the Father. "Whoever has seen me has seen the Father" (John 14:9), he told them. "Very truly, I tell you, the one who believes in me will also do the works that I do and, in fact, will do greater works than these, because I am going to the Father. I will do whatever you ask in my name, so that the Father may be glorified in the Son. If in my name you ask me for anything, I will do it" (John 14:12-14).

What a startling claim! What an amazing promise! What a testimony to the power of prayer, a power that Jesus offered his disciples, a power that he offers to *us*! In Jesus Christ we are free to pray! Hear his words: "Very truly, I tell you, if you ask anything of the Father in my name, he will give it to you.... Ask and you will receive, so that your joy may be complete" (John 16:23-24). "Whatever you ask in prayer, you will receive, if you have faith" (Matthew 21:22) — if you have faith, faith in God.

So the question is, Do you really believe in God, a personal God, a God who hears and answers prayers? The underlying motive for prayer should be our sincere love for God, which prompts us to express our joy and thanksgiving for God's blessings, and our concern for our fellow human beings, which moves us to petition God in their behalf. Do you really love God?

And do you believe that the nature, purpose, and power of God have been revealed to us in Jesus Christ? It is to those who believe in him that Jesus offers this tremendous power of prayer. He invites us to ask all things in his name. We are free to address God not as the Great Unknown, not as Infinite Mind, not as a Universal Principle or Plato's Idea of the Good, but as our Heavenly Father. "Pray then in this way, he said: "Our Father in heaven, hallowed be thy name" (Matthew 6:9; cf. Luke 11:2).

We Christians have no monopoly on prayer, of course. Devout Muslims put most Christians to shame, when it comes to prayer. All God-fearing people cherish the right to pray. They acknowledge prayer to be an indispensable corollary of human freedom. If this freedom were in jeopardy, people would suffer for it, fight for it, die for it. For many Christians, nevertheless, this cherished freedom to pray is a neglected if not an unused freedom.

Many would deny this, of course. They say their prayers at night (most of the time), say grace at meals (when they're at home), pray in church (when they go). But is this what the apostle had in mind when he told the Thessalonians to "pray without ceasing" (I Thessalonians 5:17)? Is this what Jesus meant when he told his disciples they ought always to pray (Luke 18:1)?

Do we contemporary Christians practice the presence of God the way Jesus did — every minute of his life? The way St. Francis did, as he went about helping others? Or Brother Lawrence, the little monk who washed dishes to the glory of God? Real prayer is continual communion with God. Our fellowship with God should be a constant relationship, not confined to certain times and places. Faith cannot be compartmentalized. This communion with God is the source of the power which Jesus promised, a power recognized even in psychiatry, a field where dedicated Christians do not abound. Most psychiatrists, however, acknowledge the benefits of prayer.

Why, then, is this freedom so often neglected? Part of the answer undoubtedly lies with those theories put forth by various skeptics, many of whom are sincere, but who have sought to explain prayer merely as a psychological phenomenon. George Buttrick, who wrote many years ago what is still one of my favorite books on prayer,[35] identified several of these psychologically based theories. One holds that the basic motive behind all prayer is *fear*, fear based not on faith but on superstition. Then there is the "collective soul" theory, which maintains that the God to whom a person prays is in reality only a personification of ideal humanity or of the clan or group to which the individual belongs. Another theory is that prayer is a form of autosuggestion; it is talking to oneself, deceiving oneself. Still another theory that is popular with unbelieving psychologists is that prayer is merely wishful thinking, a projection of one's desires upon a god whose only reality is in our mind.

While it is possible to refute these arguments against prayer, there is ultimately no argument *for* prayer except praying. The arguments against prayer are always put forth by non-praying individuals. That is like a tone-deaf rock-and-roller trying to disprove the beauty of Brahm's *Second Symphony*. It is interesting that Jesus did not set about proving the reality of prayer. He merely asserted what prayer can do. He based his claims on the presuppositions that human beings are free and that God is personal.

Any person of faith can understand that. Anyone who has experienced personal communion with God does not have to prove the value of prayer to oneself or to anyone else. Indeed, one cannot prove it, any more than one can "prove" the reality of the love one feels for another person. The warrior skeptics, nevertheless, continue to hurl their intellectual spears, and undoubtedly they have taken their toll.

The cynics and skeptics are not the main reason we do not exercise our freedom to pray, however. Rather it is our own spiritual indifference, or laziness. We're just too tired, or too busy to pray. That can be just as true of us ministers as of the lay folks we are always urging to pray, a thought that led to me to wonder:

If prayer is essential,
in tough times like these,
why aren't more clergy trousers
worn out at the knees?[36]

Underlying the indifference of many people is probably a lack of confidence in themselves and in God. They feel they just don't know how to pray. They're not sure what to say or how to say it. And behind their self-consciousness is lurking the doubt that maybe God, if there is a personal God, "won't hear me anyway, and even if God does hear, God probably can't really answer me, at least not the way I want."

Obviously, if we are to avail ourselves of our freedom to pray, we must understand *how* to pray, and to understand how to pray we must know what prayer is and what it can do. In his letter to the Philippians, Paul wrote: "Do not worry about anything, but in everything by prayer and supplication with thanksgiving let your requests be made known to God" (Philippians 4:6). Paul exhorts us to tell God the desires of our hearts. We have the freedom to petition God in prayer, and that means for material as well as for spiritual things! In the prayer Jesus taught his disciples, which we call "the Lord's Prayer," we pray for our daily bread (Matthew 6:11; Luke 11:3).

"In everything let your requests be made known to God." God's grace is ours for the asking! We are free to seek God's help in all things. Petition is an integral part of prayer. We pray for forgiveness; that's a petition. When we pray for good health, long life, peace, patience, courage, strength, or guidance, these are all petitions. When we pray for others, asking God to heal the sick, comfort the afflicted, support the weak, these, too, are petitions. Every intercessory prayer is a petition. With all the problems there are in the world today, we have much to bring before God in our intercessory prayers. Some petitions are less worthy than others, of course, like that of the man who prayed, "If somebody has to be poor, O God, just don't let it be me. Amen."

We are free to ask God to make us rich, but that doesn't mean it's right. And we must realize that God does not always answer our prayers as we expect. God always answers our prayers, but

God doesn't always grant our requests. Sometimes the answer is Yes, sometimes No, and sometimes Not Yet. So we must pray with intelligence, as well as with faith, remembering that in Christ we are also free to think (see Chapter 11). One of our petitions should always be for the wisdom to discern God's answers to our prayers. God might make us rich by teaching us there are things of greater value than money.

If God knows our needs better than we ourselves, even before we ask, why do we need to pray? Prayer is necessary because it is our pipe-line to God. We were created for eternal fellowship with God. Prayer is our conversation with God. It is a two-way conversation, not a soliloquy or a monologue. That requires listening on our part, as well as speaking (see Chapter 7). When we pray, we give the Holy Spirit a chance to work in our hearts.

With what attitude should we pray? The apostle Paul said "by prayer and supplication with thanksgiving" make your requests known. Supplication is humble and earnest prayer. One cannot commune with God without a sense of humility. To pray with humility is to recognize that God knows our needs and others' needs better than we do. We acknowledge that, when we pray "Nevertheless, not my will but thy will be done." Praying with humility means praying submissively. Pray with humility, says Paul.

And pray with thanks. Thanksgiving is the fountainhead of all prayer, for it is the spontaneous expression of our gratitude for all that God has done for us. One of the best ways to get in the mood for prayer is to count your blessings. As one of the old gospel songs puts it, "Count your blessings, name them one by one, and it will surprise you what the Lord has done."[37]

We must pray with humility and thankfulness, and with joy. Paul exhorts us to "Rejoice in the Lord always" (Philippians 4:4). This is the keynote of his letters, all but one of which begin with praise and rejoicing for God's blessings. To the Philippians he writes, "I thank my God every time I remember you, constantly praying with joy in every one of my prayers..." (1:3-4).

So let us be joyful, and let us be natural. We need erect no psychological barriers because of any inability to use highfalutin theological language. We owe God our best thought, that is true.

But we can express our thoughts in our own words. The language of prayer is always beautiful when it comes from the heart, like that of a friend of mine whose first words each morning are, "Thank you, Lord, for another day. May I live it to your glory."

This kind of prayer is the solution to our human anxiety. Paul says have no anxiety about anything. That is why psychologists view prayer as an effective emotional release. Prayer is not the result of our anxiety but the answer to it. "Cast all your anxiety on him," wrote Peter, "because he cares for you" (I Peter 5:7). Prayer is not the result of fear but a means of helping us overcome fear. "The Lord is my helper; I will not be afraid" (Hebrew 13:6).

So to one who is worried, frustrated, confused, anxious, afraid, the best advice is what is often sung but not so often heeded, "Take it to the Lord in prayer."[38] Are you going through an emotional crisis? Take it to the Lord in prayer. Are you discouraged or depressed? "Do not let your hearts be troubled, and do not let them be afraid," said Jesus (John 14:27b). "Have no anxiety about anything, but in everything by prayer and supplication with thanksgiving let your requests be made known to God" (Philippians 4:6, R.S.V).

And if you do this, what then? Then "the peace of God, which surpasses all understanding, will guard your hearts and your minds in Christ Jesus" (Philippians 4:7). This is the effect of prayer. This is what it can do for you. Instead of anxiety you will know the peace of God, a peace that passes all human understanding. A psychiatrist can help someone who is emotionally disturbed, for God wants us to combat mental illness just as we try to deal with every other human sickness. But one may be cured by a psychiatrist and still not have the peace of God. That kind of peace is found only in the life of prayer, a life which results in the equanimity known by those who live in fellowship with God through Christ. This is what Paul meant by being in Christ Jesus. It is a perfect unity of spirit, a oneness which can be maintained only by prayer.

We have to cultivate the prayer habit. That does not mean that prayer should be a mechanical, unthinking act. The prayer habit is never routine. It requires all the concentration, all the attentiveness we possess. That's what Paul meant when he told the Colossians, "Devote yourselves to prayer, keeping alert in it..." (Colossians 4:2).

To develop the habit of prayer one needs to have regular times for praying. That would certainly include starting the day with a prayer, even it if is only a very short one. I think it is a good idea to say a brief prayer before you get out of bed in the morning, thanking God for a new day and asking God to be with you and to guide you throughout the day. We should let our first thoughts each day be of God.

Similarly, we should end the day with a prayer, giving thanks for God's blessings, asking forgiveness for whatever wrongs we may have committed or mistakes we have made, lifting up to God our special needs, and sharing with God the hopes and fears, joys and sorrows we are feeling at the time. In addition to morning and bedtime prayers, we can also pray at mealtimes, whether we are at home or in a public restaurant. This can be a spoken or a silent grace, with our eyes open or closed, but we need to make it a habit to ask God's blessing at every meal.

Already this would be five prayer times a day, a good start toward developing the habit of prayer. In addition to these times, there should also be a quiet time during the day, a few moments set apart, when we pause and give God a chance to speak to us. You might be thinking, "How can I do that, when I'm in an office all day, surrounded by people? When can I ever have a quiet time?" Maybe not during your working hours, but surely sometime during the day you could spare a few minutes for God. It's a matter of self-discipline. If you think of all the reasons you can't, then you won't. But if you really want to, you can. You can pray on your way home. You can stare out the window of the bus and think about God. I like to pray when I'm driving alone in a car. As a last resort, you can combine your quiet time with your bedtime prayer. Ideally, the quiet time should include some Bible reading, a time of reflection on the Scripture passage, and finally prayer.

Finding a regular time may be hard at first, but continue steadfastly until it becomes a habit. When this happens, prayer comes much more naturally on other occasions. You'll find yourself frequently offering up mini-prayers of thanksgiving for the evidences of God's providential care and gracious working in your life. You'll turn to God more readily in time of joy, or sorrow, or trouble. You'll thank God for a safe trip, or ask God's guidance in some important decision, or beg God's forgiveness for a slip of the tongue. Prayer thus becomes a way of life. It's more an attitude than an act.

In these few pages I cannot hope to do justice to the subject of prayer. It is a huge topic. I have several shelves full of books on prayer and the devotional life. In keeping with the theme of this book my focus here has been on prayer as an essential element of the freedom to which we are called in Christ. Notwithstanding that limited aspect, I should like to offer just a few practical suggestions on learning to pray, for those who might be new to the practice.

The best way to develop the language of prayer and to increase your comfort level with it is to write out what you want to say. Put your ideas down in writing. It's an excellent discipline, which will help you sharpen your prayers.

A second helpful practice is one I have already mentioned: pray aloud alone. Many people are frightened at the thought of having to pray aloud in public. What's the remedy? Pray aloud when there is no one else around to hear you, no one but God. I know of no better way to overcome one's fear of praying in public. Incidentally, when Jesus talked about praying in secret, he was not condemning the idea of praying with others, something he himself often did. What he condemned was the hypocrisy of those who make a display of their piety. Praying aloud when you are by yourself will make it easier to pray aloud with and for others.

It offers the further advantage of keeping your mind from wandering. I know my thoughts can begin to stray after I've been praying a while, but not when I'm praying aloud. For that reason I've made a habit of praying aloud most of the time, softly but audibly. It's wonderful the way the Holy Spirit puts the words on your lips, so that you feel almost as if you are speaking God's thoughts back to God. It's a thrilling experience when that happens, and I think it has helped me more than anything else in learning to pray.

My third suggestion is to have a prayer list. Without one I can't possibly remember all the people for whom I want to pray and ought to pray. As a pastor I always used the church directory as an intercessory prayer list. If you know people's needs you can be very specific. Otherwise, you can simply ask God, for example, to help them be better persons, better Christians, and to attend to all their needs as God knows best. You will find your intercessory prayer list can expand very quickly.

I would also recommend praying with others, whenever you have the opportunity. It's wonderful when spouses can be prayer partners. Prayer partners not only stimulate each other's spiritual growth, as they learn from one another and share with one another the evidences of God's working in their lives, but they also encourage each other to keep at it. Praying with others helps everyone to feel more comfortable with praying aloud, and it teaches the participants in dramatic ways what prayer can do.

My fifth suggestion is to use some devotional aids to stimulate, enrich, and guide your prayer life. The Bible, needless to say, is indispensable. Work the language of the Psalms and other biblical passages into your own prayers. In addition, there are many beautiful prayer books and books about prayer. Every good hymn book is filled with beautiful prayers. Learn to read the great hymns of the church as prayers. The more prayers you read, the more familiar you become with the language of prayer and the easier it will be to express your own thoughts in prayer.

Not that prayer itself will ever be "easy," for it is often a struggle even for the most devout disciples. There are times when you may feel you are not getting through to God, times when your mind is so cluttered with your own thoughts that you can't concentrate on God, times when you just don't feel like praying. But those are just the times you should pray, because those are often the times you need God the most. It's part of the discipline of prayer, and you should never allow your prayer life to depend on your moods. Your feelings have very little to do with your need of prayer.

What is called for is diligence. You have to keep at it, whether you feel like it or not. It also calls for sincerity. If you don't feel like praying, you can begin by admitting that to God. Some of my best prayer times have been when I have felt least like praying. Maybe that's because at times like that I am most dependent upon and open to God. Being sincere means being honest with God, saying what's really on your heart. God knows our hearts, and God answers our dominant desires. It also means being natural, as I have already mentioned. Be yourself. Don't try to be somebody else. God knows who you are.

It takes courage to ask God for the things you know you really need but are afraid to ask for, like the willingness to forgive someone who has offended you, the capacity to love someone you don't like, the strength to overcome some temptation. Do you have the courage to ask God to help you break some bad habit or addiction? Do you trust God enough to accept God's answer to your prayer? It takes courage to pray submissively. It takes courage to pray "Thy will be done" and really mean it.

It also takes confidence in God's goodness and grace. You must believe that God answers the prayers of believers. For God does answer our prayers, when we pray in Jesus' name. That doesn't mean just saying Jesus' name. It means praying as one who bears the name of Christ, praying in the spirit with which Jesus prayed, the spirit in which he lived and died. If you pray as Jesus prayed, you can be confident that God will answer your prayer, and in a way that with the hindsight of faith you will know is good. You will be able to say with Paul, "In everything God works for good with those who love God and are called according to God's purpose" (Romans 8:28).

"More things are wrought by prayer than this world dreams of," said Tennyson.[39] For anyone who is in Christ, not to pray would be like going without food. Without a steady diet of prayer one will suffer from spiritual malnutrition. Furthermore, if God desires our prayers, for us *not* to pray is a sin. If we don't pray, we close the door on the friendship which Christ offers us.

When we fail to pray for others, we neglect not only them, but Christ. When the people of Israel asked Samuel to intercede for them to God because of their sin, he said, "Far be it from me that I should sin against the LORD by ceasing to pray for you" (I Samuel 12:23). For Samuel not to pray for the people would have been a sin. He was their priest, and in Christ you and I have been made priests to one another.

Prayer is the adhesive that knits us together in true Christian fellowship. Prayer is the language of faith. It is the source of our power, the well spring of our peace. As James Montgomery puts it in his beautiful hymn,

> *Prayer is the soul's sincere desire,*
> *   unuttered or expressed,*
> *the motion of a hidden fire*
> *   that trembles in the breast.*
> *Prayer is the burden of a sigh,*
> *   the falling of a tear,*
> *the upward glancing of an eye,*
> *   when none but God is near.*[40]

The freedom for which Christ has set us free includes the freedom to pray. To commune with God is a sacred privilege. How can any believer not use that precious gift?

Questions For Personal Reflection
And/Or Group Discussion

1. Do you believe God hears and answers your prayers? Why do you or don't you?

2. In a typical day, how much time do you spend in prayer? Do you feel you have to be "in the mood" to pray? If so, when do you feel most like praying? Where and how do you pray? Do you prefer to pray alone or with others?

3. What does it mean to you to pray in Jesus' name?

4. Write a prayer expressing your gratitude to God for as many things as you can think of.

5. For whom do you or should you pray and what do you ask God to do for others? How have you prayed following some great national tragedy?

6. Write a brief prayer of invocation that could be used at a community testimonial dinner for the retiring president of the local bank. Now try writing a brief prayer of confession for use by a congregation in public worship.

Chapter Ten

The Real Me
Free To Be Ourselves

"I am what I am." These words became a household saying two generations ago because of the well-known movie cartoon character, "Popeye, the sailor man." Their children watched the same cartoons on television, and not too many years ago Robin Williams starred in a movie version of "Popeye." There are not many adults of any age today who would not recognize the familiar theme-song of the jaunty, one-eyed, spinach-loving hero: "I yam what I yam, and that's all I yam, I'm Popeye the sailor man." Popeye and his perpetual sweetheart Olive Oyle probably never realized that his favorite saying had a sound Biblical precedent, for the same thought was uttered long ago by a far greater figure than Popeye.

"By the grace of God," declared the apostle Paul, "I am what I am." This line from Paul's first letter to the church at Corinth (v15:10) is a revealing statement, for it shows that Paul had discovered the importance of being himself. What's so important about that, you ask? What else could he be but himself?

He could have been, as so many of us are, something less than he was meant to be. It is ironic that what should be the easiest and most natural thing is actually the most difficult for many people. That's because they spend their lives trying to be somebody other than themselves. They would not admit that, of course, even if they were aware of it. But the truth is that many people spend much of their energy trying to conform to the image they have created for themselves, or which someone else has created for them, instead of being the person God intended them to be. They feel they must be somebody different from the person they really are, a compulsion which if over indulged can result in all sorts of inner tension

97

and turmoil, unnatural behavior, aimless activity, arrested personality development, and even serious emotional disorders.

The freedom for which Christ has set us free should surely include the freedom to be ourselves, our very best selves, but this may be our most neglected freedom. Too many people spend most of their lives hiding behind the masks they fashion for themselves, never daring to reveal themselves, their *real* selves, to the people around them. They are not real persons; they are human chameleons, striving desperately to blend with the color of their environment, animated manikins adapting themselves to the shifting patterns of their social milieu.

Yet everybody talks about the importance of being a real person. To be a phoney is about the worst thing one can be. One has to be *real*. One's major task is to be oneself, one's true self. But how does one go about being one's true self? You cannot *be* yourself until you *accept* yourself, and you can't accept yourself until you *know* yourself. The first requirement, then, is to know yourself. By that I mean discovering what you're meant to be. Am I a real person, a fully developed personality, or am I less than I ought to be? Am I "what I am," or am I something else?

One important aspect of self-identity is a person's occupation. When groups of strangers gather, I've noticed they often describe themselves by announcing what they do for a living. It's usually the first thing they tell about themselves, after they say their name, as they introduce themselves around the circle at a seminar, for instance. "I'm Maria Sanchez; I'm an architect ... I'm Y. T. Lee; I'm retired."

If that's the case, then part of being the self you were meant to be should include doing what you were meant to do. If you believe in God, that discovery must take place in the realm of faith. It's the difference between an occupation and a vocation, between viewing your work as a job or as a calling.

Take Paul, for example. He discovered God wanted him to be an apostle. The discovery came in a dramatic and compelling way, when he met the risen Christ on the road to Damascus. From that point on Paul's whole life was changed. He knew what he was meant to be. From then on he would introduce himself as Paul, an apostle of Jesus Christ.

Most of us, of course, do not have the advantage of a life-changing vision such as Paul had. Our self-discovery must come in less dramatic ways. But it is still possible for us to know ourselves. It requires some critical self-examination and lots of prayer. There is a healthy kind of prayerful introspection which enables one to assess one's life from time to time, to add up one's personal (not material) assets and liabilities. If I'm employed, am I doing the work God's wants me to do? If I'm retired, am I still a good steward of the time God has given me? Am I utilizing my abilities to the fullest possible extent? —in accordance with God's purpose for my life today?

I believe that one who is fortunate enough to live in a free country and who is not the helpless victim of poverty or disease, can find one's proper niche, if one sincerely seeks God's will for one's life. It may mean a drastic revision of one's plans, as it did for Paul. From being a persecutor of the church he became its leading missionary. For a person today it may mean a change of habits or a change of jobs, as it did for me. It was not that my old job was bad, but that I had found a new calling. My old occupation had been replaced by a new vocation.

More important than the occupational changes that might occur are the effects that self-discovery has upon personality development and character. What kind of a person am I really? Am I living a sham existence, trying to fool somebody or everybody, including myself, putting on airs, speaking and acting for effect only? My attempts to be open to others often fall short. Even my confessions sometimes sound more like explanations than admissions, more like self-compliments than confessions. I call them self-justifying confessions.

I'm not referring to the kind of confession discussed in Chapter 8. I'm talking about the kind I have read in the dossiers of ministerial candidates, when they are asked to indicate their personal strengths and weaknesses. The latter call for some honest introspection, but more often than not what is meant to be a confessional statement is intended to evoke not constructive criticism but sympathy or admiration. "My main weakness is that I work too hard.... My weakness is that I take my ministry too seriously.... I know I care too much about people and consequently I sometimes get hurt ..." etc., etc. Self-justifying confessions!

To discover my true self requires seeing through the veneer of my outward appearance. How much am I stunted by social pressures? Have I accepted my limitations? Am I overly concerned with the impression I make? What are my real strengths, my real weaknesses, my shortcomings? Paul knew his. He said "I am the least of the apostles, unfit to be called an apostle, because I persecuted the church of God." No self-justification there!

Nevertheless, Paul did not give up on himself, for he knew himself to be called by God, and for that reason he was free to accept himself. "By the grace of God I am what I am." If God called Paul to be an apostle, despite his past, why should Paul not accept himself? Because God had forgiven him, he was free to forgive himself. Paul admitted his apostleship was not granted on the basis of merit, but by the grace of God. How else could such a transformation have taken place? How else could this arch-enemy of the Christians, this brilliant Pharisee who had so zealously persecuted the followers of Jesus, have suddenly become Christ's greatest ambassador? How else can one explain this amazing transformation?

Think what Paul had to overcome: years of training and mental conditioning, a way of life, a way of thinking. Imagine the ridicule he received from his former colleagues among the Pharisees. Imagine the suspicion of those who remembered his earlier cruelties. How they must have taunted him, forever bringing up the past. Despite all this, Paul discovered he was meant to be something else and he accepted it. He accepted himself because God in Christ had accepted him. Paul could have refused to accept his acceptance. He could have rationalized. "I, Paul, become a Christian? Preposterous! I, Paul an apostle? Ridiculous!"

How tempted we can be to react this way when God speaks to us through someone else. We try to put the thought out of our mind, or think of reasons why we shouldn't be or do what the Holy Spirit is nudging us to be or do. We rationalize why we shouldn't accept

God's call to be our true selves. But not Paul: "I was not disobedient to the heavenly vision," he declared. He accepted himself, the self he was called to be.

One cannot *be* oneself, until one *accepts* oneself. The inner conflict that rages between the self we want to be and the self we think we are, can be resolved only when we accept the self we are and live with it. We must be willing to say, as Paul said, "I am what I am." But we must say it in the same spirit as Paul said it. It is not a negative but a positive statement. It's not an excuse for condoning our shortcomings, nor is it a boast. It is simply a declaration of acceptance.

Some people cannot make such a declaration because they are too dissatisfied with themselves. The discrepancy between who they are and who they think they should be is too great. For this reason a woman of great ability may be unable to accept herself because she has set her standards unreasonably high, while an ignorant laggard with no ambition whatsoever may be quite content with himself. The need for self-acceptance, nevertheless, is basic for all of us, and it can be a problem for the fortunate as well as for the underprivileged.

When their feeling of inadequacy becomes too strong, people deal with it in ways that are sometimes unhealthy, sometimes even violent. We are shocked when some disturbed youth or adult goes on a shooting rampage, randomly killing people. Why do they do it, we ask? Is it partly their way of dealing with their own failures, their own feeling of rejection? Do they hate themselves so much that they have to vent their rage on others, often including their own family?

Fortunately most people do not resort to such violent extremes in order to cover up their own insecurities. Some people do it by adopting a braggadocio attitude. Their swaggering false front masks their inferiority complex. Others divert attention from their own deficiencies by criticizing those who have the strengths they themselves lack, or by belittling the importance of those strengths.

Then there are the Walter Mitty[41] types who live in a dream world of their own making, one in which they can pretend to be whatever they fantasize. Still others do just the opposite and excuse themselves by exaggerating their inferiority, thus exonerating themselves from all responsibility. "I just can't do anything right!" That's supposed to explain every failure.

All these ways of dealing with inferiority are attempts to achieve self-acceptance by deception. The result is not a true self at all, but a pretender. To be oneself one must accept oneself as is and go on from there. Whatever one's handicaps, whatever one's limitations, one accepts them and tries to make the best of them.

Ironically, that means acknowledging our deceptive ways. Accepting ourselves means accepting ourselves masks and all! Who is the real me? It is the good me *and* the bad me, the true me *and* the false me. It is the me I hide and the me I reveal, the me I am and the me I pretend to be. That pretense, that very phoniness, is part of my reality, too!

This brings us to the final step in being oneself, which is simply *to be oneself*. Having discovered oneself and accepted oneself, there remains but the direction of one's whole energies to giving that self full expression. It is to follow the advice of Polonius to his son Laertes: "This above all, to thine own self be true, and it must follow, as the night the day, thou canst not be false to any man."[42]

"I am the least of the apostles.... But by the grace of God I am what I am," said Paul, "and God's grace toward me has not been in vain. On the contrary, I worked harder than any of them — though it was not I, but the grace of God that is with me" (I Corinthians 15:9-10). One must work at being oneself. It is not easy. Handicapped persons can lead useful, meaningful lives, but they have to work at it. The mature person is the one who views one's handicaps as obstacles to be overcome, not as stumbling blocks but as stepping stones to a fuller, more rewarding life.

I think of all the athletes I have known or read about who overcame physical handicaps to become champions in sports in which one would think they could never even participate, let alone excel. Psychologists call it over-compensating. As someone who has played the piano all his life but never very well, I marvel at the stories of people like Alec Templeton, George Shearing, and Ray Charles, each of whom became a great pianist, though totally blind.

I think of Helen Keller, born deaf, dumb, and blind, but who, thanks to the patience and love of a devoted nanny, was able to become the person she was meant to be.

The apostle Paul had his thorn in the flesh, too, but it did not prevent him from accomplishing all that he did. Why? Because his strength was in Christ. "I can do all things through him who strengthens me," he declared (Philippians 4:13).

So, too, the mistakes of our past can be turned to future gain, if they are properly dealt with. What counts is not what we've done in the past, but what we expect to do with our lives in the future. You can't be yourself if you're living in the past, whether the past is good or bad. In Jesus Christ we are free to remember the past, not to remain in it!

Paul had persecuted the church, but that was no reason for shirking his mission. Instead, his preaching became all the more effective because of the very fact he had been a persecutor before. So, too, today the most convincing Christians are those whose lives have been transformed by the gospel, and for me the most moving testimonies are those of individuals who have been lifted out of the mire of sin. In Christ they have been freed from any debilitating guilt complex. The reality of their past mistakes is a motive not for giving up but for giving out.

Being oneself means striving to overcome our handicaps, profiting from our past mistakes, and channeling our energies toward worthy goals. There are those who think being oneself means being uninhibited, being willing to let one's hair down, enjoying one's natural urges. On the contrary, it means self-discipline. It means containing our natural drives and putting them to work for higher purposes. We are more than animals. We are human beings created in the image of God to have fellowship with God.

One of my favorite movies of all time is *The African Queen*. It's one of the classic films that I enjoy watching periodically. There's a delightful scene in which Mr. Allnut, played by Humphrey Bogart, is complaining about the efforts of Rose, the spinster daughter of a missionary, to reform him of his minor vices. "So I drink a little too much once in a while — it's only human nature!" complains Mr. Allnut. Whereupon Rose, played by Katherine Hepburn, replies: "Nature, Mr. Allnut, is what we are put on this earth to rise above."

To be the person God intended me to be, my true self, I must understand that I am ultimately responsible to God and must live my life accordingly. In Jesus Christ I am free to know myself, free to accept myself; free to be myself. I am free not only to know myself, but to know myself to be a child of God made in God's image and responsible to God. I am free not only to accept myself, but to accept myself knowing that God has accepted me and has demonstrated it supremely in the death of God's Son on the cross. I am free not only be myself, but free to be the self I was intended to be, holy and acceptable to God, which is my reasonable service (Romans 12:1).

Not that I'll ever fully arrive. Being oneself is a never-ceasing process of growth. It is a state of becoming. Paul expressed it beautifully in his letter to the Philippians: "Not that I have already obtained this or have already reached the goal; but I press on to make it my own, because Christ Jesus has made me his own. Beloved, I do not consider that I have made it my own; but this one thing I do: forgetting what lies behind and straining forward to what lies ahead, I press on toward the goal for the prize of the heavenly call of God in Christ Jesus. Let those of us then who are mature be of the same mind..." (3:12-15).

Here's another way of expressing our self-identity struggle:

> *God created me. I don't understand —*
> *is what I am now the "me" that God planned?*
> *If by the Lord's grace I am what I am,*
> *can I be to blame, whatever I am?*
> *Is claiming that just a pretext to say*
> *whatever I am is really okay?*
> *As if what I am is not up to me?*
> *So blame it on God, and I go Scot free!*
> *Or does God alone observe the real me,*
> *not just what I am, but what I can be?*
> *God knows my desires as well as my needs.*
> *God knows the intent behind all my deeds.*

The "me" others know is not the real me;
nor is it the "me" I want them to see.
I'm not what I seem. Yet is it not true,
that masquerade "me" is part of me, too?
Beneath the facades the world need not see;
the masks that I choose reveal the real me!
Indeed, I confess that it may well be
those phoney facades are closest to me.
To know who I am may be but a sham.
Salvation is this: to know <u>whose</u> I am,
to know I am Christ's by grace and that he
can free me through faith to be the real me.[43]

Questions For Personal Reflection
And/Or Group Discussion

1. Does anyone know the real you? Who do you think knows you better than anyone else does? Why do you feel that person understands you?

2. How would you describe "the real you"? Do you like "the real you"? Why?

3. When do you most feel as if you are "being yourself"? With whom are you most comfortable being yourself?

4. Can you think of things you do to keep people from knowing the real you? What are some of the masks you wear at times?

5. Can you tell when another person is being himself or herself (i.e., the real person)? How can you tell? How does your awareness affect the way you relate to that person?

6. Do you believe that Jesus Christ can free you to be the person you want to be? How would you like him to help you?

Chapter Eleven

Let X Equal The Unknown Quantity
Free To Think

The ability to think is a fascinating phenomenon. Attempts to explain the cognitive process can be traced all the way back to Plato and Aristotle. In our time cognitive psychologists have used computer concepts such as coding, storing, and retrieving information, to describe the functions of the human brain. The developing field of neuroscience is studying the human nervous system, the brain, and the biological basis of consciousness, perception, memory, and learning. The findings are often controversial, but one that intrigues me is that, contrary to what many people have been led to believe, the human brain does not function like a computer. It changes with use. The brain is a self-organizing system of some ten billion neurons with a quadrillion connections and something like ten to the millionth power possible combinations of connections. Such staggering figures are beyond my comprehension.

After skimming through some of the writings of theorists like Thorndike, Ruger, Watson, Freud, Köhler, Spearmand, and Piaget, I am more confused than informed. The Gestalt psychologists have one approach. The Freudian School has another. While it is a fascinating study, one is left with the conviction that despite the persistent experiments in this field and the increasing knowledge of the various parts of the brain and their functions, our contemporary understanding of the human thought processes is still very limited. There has been progress, of course, but despite all the work being done by psychologists, physiologists, anthropologists, linguists, and others in all the related disciplines in the exploding field of cognitive research, much about the nature of human thinking remains an unfathomed mystery. If the scientists in their various fields of expertise can't solve the mystery, the average lay person like me certainly cannot hope to do so.

But one can at least begin with the general observation that part of the human species' superiority over the other creatures has to do with our greater reasoning powers. Although Wolfgang Köhler, the founder of Gestalt psychology, demonstrated that some animals are capable of exhibiting considerable insight, they are far below human beings in thinking power. Köhler conducted a famous experiment with an ape, in which some food was placed outside of the cage and just beyond the reach of the beast. After considerable frustration, the ape was able to devise a tool long enough to reach the food by fitting several short bamboo sticks together, one inside the another.

There is no doubt that the ape was thinking, but I for one am not willing to concede that the most intelligent chimpanzee can be measured on the same intellectual scale with a human being, despite the many jokes to the contrary. There is the familiar one, for example, about the chimpanzee that had been taught to read and write. On completion of Darwin's *Origin of the Species* the chimp exclaimed: "Good heavens! Am I my keeper's brother?"

Notwithstanding such humorous references to animal intelligence, we human beings are endowed with a capacity to reason quite distinct from that of any other living creature. We have the unique ability to think in abstractions. We can observe hypothetical relationships. Can you picture a chimpanzee saying, "Let X equal the unknown quantity"?

Our ability to do complex reasoning is indeed a distinguishing characteristic of the human species. The French philosopher Rene Descartes even used it as the theoretical proof of his existence: "*Cogito ergo sum*"— I think, therefore I am.[44] "The power of thought, the magic of the mind" mused Lord Byron the poet.[45]

How curious that human beings, who have been given this amazing ability, this incredible power to think, make so little use of it! To paraphrase Mark Twain's comment about the weather, everyone talks about thinking but few people do any of it! Perish the thought, we say — and how it does! Thoughtless behavior, thoughtless words. How often we tend to speak and act first, and think afterwards. Some people *try* to think, some people *think* they think, but most people seldom think. "Few people think more than two or three times a year," commented George Bernard Shaw; "I have made an international reputation by thinking once or twice a week." And Jane Taylor, in her *Essays in Rhyme*, wrote:

> *Though man a thinking being is defined,*
> *few use the grand prerogative of mind.*
> *How few think justly of the thinking few!*
> *How many never think, who think they do!*[46]

No wonder Thomas Carlyle asked, "In every epoch of the world, the great event, parent of all others, is it not the arrival of a Thinker in the world?"[47]

Two thousand years ago there lived one such person whose thinking transformed the world. His name was Jesus. He performed miracles of healing. He taught as no other person has ever taught. He spoke as no other human being has ever dared to speak. He was a man of action, a man of prayer, a man of thought.

How often we overlook the emphasis which Jesus placed upon right thinking. "You shall love the Lord your God with all your heart, and with all your soul, *and with all your mind,*" he said (Matthew 22:37). We have a responsibility to use our God-given ability to think, a duty to serve God with our minds. As I have already said, Christianity is a thinking person's faith.[48] It challenges our intellect as well as our will.

Thinking is more than an obligation on our part, however. It is a glorious privilege! For freedom Christ has set us free to think! That means we have the freedom to ask questions, the freedom to search and to probe, the freedom to voice our doubts and uncertainties. It means, too, that our faith is intellectually tenable, that it will withstand the closest scrutiny, bear the finest examination, reward the most serious study.

Let no one suppose that Christianity is not an intellectual challenge. Take the Bible as a case in point. The Bible is a difficult book, one reason being that it doesn't always mean what it says. That reality prompted this poem:

Oh, the Bible is a challenge to the mind, to the mind;
it's a challenge to the mind and to the heart.
If you listen to the Spirit, when you read it, you will find,
that to take it word for word is not too smart.
For it doesn't always mean just what it says, what it says,
but the Bible always means just what it means.
Any person who can read it can tell others what it says,
but the test is to interpret what it means!
So to quote a Scripture passage may not be the wisest way,
if the context of the passage isn't clear.
Any text without a context is a proof text, as they say.
That's what's wrong with some theology we hear![49]

So the Bible is not for the simple-minded. It is not a children's book. On the contrary, the Bible is very much an adult book. Its meaning can be explained to children, of course, but it must be interpreted, put into language they can understand. And for adults it must be systematically studied to be understood. There are many parts of the Bible that no one can really understand, passages about which the commentators and biblical scholars disagree, passages where the student can only make an intelligent guess as to the meaning.

On the other hand, there are many passages where the meaning is quite clear, verses which speak with power and clarity to the hearts of believers, as they read the holy book devotionally. We have to learn to distinguish between the various parts of the Bible, know where to go for help in understanding it, and by all means have a disciplined program of Bible study. That is, if we sincerely want to fulfill Jesus' command to love God with all our mind. If we want to know God, we have to know the Bible, and if we want to know the Bible, we have to study it.

What increases the challenge of understanding the Bible is the fact that the Bible often raises more questions than it answers. This is due to the element of mystery in our faith, an element which should always keep us humble. Because the Bible does not contain direct answers to many of the questions we ask, it is the role of theology to examine, to interpret, to define, and to apply the principles of our faith. Theology is the church speaking to itself, an ongoing process of self-analysis and introspection, the object of which is to make possible more effective and relevant communication of the gospel to each generation.

The good news of Jesus Christ does not change, but language and thought patterns do change, and the gospel must be continually reinterpreted and restated to each age. Thus we have a tremendous task to apply our best thought to our faith, ever seeking to increase our understanding and knowledge of Christ. Christianity is indeed a thinking person's faith.

Unfortunately, however, we must admit that many of us do not always use our freedom to think about our faith, and some people never do. Maybe they're too lazy or too afraid to think. Maybe they're afraid there might not be answers to the questions they're afraid to ask. How could Jesus be both human and divine? How do we know the things he said about himself are true? Was he really born of a virgin, or is that just one of those things we're supposed to accept on faith? Do we have to believe in his so-called miracles? If he really was God's Son, why did he have to die? Why would God let the Son of God suffer and be killed? What really happened that first Easter morning? Can't I believe in God without believing in Jesus? What does it mean to be saved? Why do we need a Savior anyway? If there is a God, and if God is good, why is there so much suffering and evil in the world? What happens when we die? Is there really a heaven? How can we believe in "the resurrection of the body"? And if there's a heaven, is there also a hell?

Have you ever thought about these kinds of questions? Have you ever really tried to find answers to some of the questions which nonbelievers often ask us? When was the last time you sat down and thought deeply about God? You shall love the Lord your God with all your mind!

But most people would say, "I do think about my faith. I do a lot of thinking." Do they? Many who think they think are often guilty of the wrong kind of thinking. There are at least four main kinds of wrong thinking, the first being *misdirected thinking*, like that of the Pharisees who tried to trap Jesus. They had obviously been thinking, when they came to Jesus to try to entangle him in his talk, but their thinking was misdirected along evil lines. Scheming is not right thinking.

The Pharisees asked Jesus a question they thought he could not answer without trapping himself. "Teacher, we know that you are sincere, and teach the way of God in accordance with truth, and show deference to no one; for you do not regard people with partiality. Tell us, then, what you think. Is it lawful to pay taxes to the emperor, or not?" (Matthew 22:16-17).

It was a devilish question. If Jesus said Yes, then he could not be their Messiah, for the Jews would not have a Messiah who would submit to the yoke of Caesar. But if he said No, then they could report him to the Roman authorities as an insurrectionist. They had him right where they wanted him, they thought.

But they didn't know the mind of the Master. Jesus saw right through the smoke screen of their phoney praise and calculated courtesy. "Jesus, aware of their malice, said, 'Why are you putting me to the test, you hypocrites? Show me the coin used for the tax'" (22:18-19). Already he had reversed the advantage, for they now had to produce the Roman coin! "Then he said to them, 'Whose head is this, and whose title?' They answered, 'The emperor's.' Then he said to them, 'Give therefore to the emperor the things that are the emperor's, and to God the things that are God's.'" In one terse sentence Jesus acknowledged their duty to the state, while affirming his deeper loyalty to God, for he and his antagonists knew that all things are God's!

Misdirected thinking in the religious sphere is a dangerous thing, and we see it today in those zealous Christians, who, motivated by a misguided zeal, preach a distorted version of the gospel, attacking those who disagree with them, and promoting hate and strife wherever they can, à la the Ku Klux Klan. Those who belong to such organizations are zealous for their cause, but their thinking is misdirected, like that of those who do violence for the cause of peace and bomb abortion clinics in the name of Jesus. They belong in the same category with the Muslim extremists who commit acts of terrorism in the name of Allah.

112

A second type of wrong thinking could be termed *unidirectional thinking*. An old-fashioned, unidirectional microphone would not pick up your voice unless you were right in front of it. Unidirectional thinking is like that. Its scope is narrow. It is preoccupied with its own pet peeves and private prejudices. Like a horse whose vision is limited by blinders, unidirectional thinking has no perspective, no peripheral vision, which our Christian faith demands of us. Instead, unidirectional thinking over-emphasizes a particular theme or idea.

So it was with the Sadducees. They, too, came to Jesus with a question they were sure he could not answer. They presented him with the problem of the woman who had been married seven times. In the resurrection, therefore, to which of her seven husbands would she be wife (Matthew 22:23-28)?

Being obsessed with their denial of the resurrection, the Sadducees had missed the whole point. "You are wrong," Jesus told them bluntly, "because you know neither the scriptures nor the power of God" (Matthew 22:29). They were applying human concepts to something beyond their earthly sphere of existence. "For in the resurrection," said Jesus, "they neither marry nor are given in marriage, but are like angels in heaven. And as for the resurrection of the dead, have you not read what was said to you by God, 'I am the God of Abraham, the God of Isaac, and the God of Jacob'? He is God not of the dead, but of the living" (Matthew 22:30-32). Thus Jesus used their own scriptures to prove to them that their forbears were still alive spiritually.

How often people are guilty of this kind of unidirectional thinking, consumed by some obsession that blinds them to the truth. They can be so single-minded that they become narrow-minded. Their minds won't open up because they're already made up. They hear everything through a sieve, rejecting or ignoring any idea that does not match their false assumptions.

Some people mistake busy-ness for thinking. They are so absorbed in their work that they become ensconced in a stuffy little oyster world of their own, with no thought for anyone or anything else. The poet Shelly was once describing his time schedule. "I study Portuguese while shaving," he said. "I translate Spanish for an hour before breakfast. I read all the forenoon and write all the afternoon; every minute of the day is filled with something." "Friend," interspersed an old Quaker who was listening, "When doth thee do thy thinking?"

Misdirected thinking, unidirected thinking, and then there is *over-directed thinking*. This is the thinking of a mind enslaved. I suspect that most of us have at times been guilty of this kind of thinking, too, when we behave like brainwashed parakeets, echoing the words of others. Oddly enough, you encounter this kind of thinking on college campuses, where conformity is king and cynical philosophers set the party line for unsophisticated students to repeat. You can lead a horse to water, but you can't make it drink. To paraphrase that familiar adage, You can send students to college, but you can't make all of them think.

Too many of our thoughts are not ours at all. Some people have about as much originality as a tape recorder. They're like the mentally retarded man who told the minister at the door of the church, "That was the worst sermon I've ever heard." The man's mother was most embarrassed by his remark, and wishing to smooth things over, she explained, "Don't pay any attention to him, Reverend. He only repeats what he hears other people say." That's an old joke, but it makes the point.

It's a sad fact that some church groups thrive on over-directed thinking. Some ecclesiastical bodies are adept at brainwashing their adherents. They don't want thinkers. They want church-going robots who think only what they're programmed to think. To question the party line is practically a capital offense.

People should not go to church to be brainwashed. They should not have to leave their minds at home on Sunday morning. Indeed, they should put on their thinking caps, when they walk into the sanctuary. The preacher has the right to tell them what they ought to think, not what they may think, and there's a big difference. We owe God our best thought. Note that it was in the context of a severe testing of his own mental powers that Jesus in reply to the lawyer's question added to the traditional commandment to love God the telling phrase "with all your *mind*."

114

Jesus, whose thinking was perfect, who time and time again had his wits tested by the most learned people of his day, who was thinking all the time, demands that we, too, love God with all our mind.

And having shown by his own example the importance of right thinking, Jesus then asked the Pharisees a question of his own. "What do you think of the Christ?" This is the crucial question, the question that each of us must answer for himself or herself. Christ doesn't ask us to tell him what our preacher thinks of him, or what the church thinks of him. He wants to know what *you* think. "What do *you* think of the Christ? Whose Son is he?"

There is yet another kind of wrong thinking, perhaps the most prevalent. Much of our thought is *undirected thinking*, the idle wandering of the mind — pointless, purposeless, powerless. We spend too much time in our world of desultory day-dreams, indulging the fanciful delights of reverie.

A little day-dreaming is relaxing and harmless, but too much undirected thought can be a sinful waste of time. In the sphere of religion it is no help toward a deeper understanding of God. Undirected thinking never comes to grips with the problems of faith, never wrestles with the vital questions of belief, never confronts the realities of living the Christian life. Undirected thinkers have a few vague notions about God, about Christ, about the church. But their faith has no real content, no meat, no substance to it. Yet some of these folks will babble on in a religious discussion, for as one poet observed, "they always talk who never think."[50]

Many Christians don't know *what* they believe — about heaven, about hell, about the devil, about the Holy Spirit, about the Church. Their reason for not asking questions is not fear but apathy. Ask them why Jesus died and they would probably say, "I don't know, I never thought about it."

"What do you think of the Christ? Whose Son is he?" "I don't know, I've never thought about it." Well, we had better think about it, because God will not settle for any fuzzy thinking. "You shall love the Lord your God with all your mind."

So the question for everyone who calls herself or himself a Christian is, What am I doing to fulfill this commandment? The church exists to help us fulfill it. The members of the nurturing, nourishing community of faith help one another to avoid undirected or misdirected thinking. Those who belong to communions with a heritage of religious freedom certainly do not believe in over-directed or unidirectional thinking. When they worship over a period of time they expect their minister to preach the whole gospel, not just one piece of it over and over again.

Of course, if they don't worship regularly, they won't hear the whole gospel. If they don't avail themselves of the opportunities to learn that the church provides through its various programs, including worship, and if they don't have a disciplined devotional life, including Bible study and prayer and discussion with other Christians, they will never be able to love God with all their mind, because they simply won't know enough.

For freedom Christ has set us free to think. What a gift! What a privilege! What a responsibility!

> *Take thou our minds, dear Lord, we humbly pray;*
> *give us the mind of Christ each passing day;*
> *teach us to know the truth that sets us free;*
> *grant us in all our thoughts to honor thee.*[51]

Questions For Personal Reflection
And/Or Group Discussion

1. What do you think it means to love God with all your mind?

2. Do you have unanswered questions about God, or Christianity, or religion in general, or any aspect of faith? If so, list as many as you can.

3. How well do you understand the Bible? Can you think of four or five specific passages that are especially difficult for you to understand? Are there parts of the Bible with which you disagree? Which parts?

4. Can you think of any examples of your own or someone else's misdirected thinking or unidirected thinking?

5. Have you experienced attempts in church, or wherever, to overdirect people's thinking? How do advertisers or political spin doctors influence your thinking? What about preachers or teachers? What about parents or friends?

6. How do Christ and the church free us from the wrong kinds of thinking? Do you feel free to love God with all your mind?

Chapter Twelve

Stumbling Blocks Or Stepping Stones?
Free To Remember

Having considered our freedom to think, it is appropriate to look next at our freedom to remember, for the memory process is indispensable to thinking. Psychologists have been studying this fascinating phenomenon for a long time. The late Dr. Karl Menninger, who with his father started the world famous Menninger Clinic and with his brother founded the renowned Menninger Foundation, concluded that the essential difference between human beings and other creatures is merely one of complexity. The memory process is far more complicated in human beings.

That being the case, we could refine our former comment about the uniqueness of our human capacity to think by saying that, despite the elephant's reputation for never forgetting, the essence of our humanity has to do with our superior ability to remember, which is the brain's capacity to store, retrieve, recognize, and re-use information. It could be the recollection of a past event ("I remember the last time you were here") or the retention of a skill ("Do you remember how to play Bridge?") or some information ("I remember the names of all the kings of Israel.") or a person ("I remember you!").

With all the scientific advances in the study of the brain, the physiology of its storage function remains a mystery. Some theorists believe there are different mechanisms and storage areas for short-term and long-term memories. The experts disagree also regarding the causes of forgetfulness, a phenomenon which everyone knows occurs very rapidly at first. Retention of information can be improved by periodically reviewing, actively recalling, and "over learning" the desired material. People also use various mnemonic devices, such as associations and symbols, to improve their retention of particular facts. Psychiatrists speak of a person's subconscious wish to forget something unpleasant. Pride, fear, or disdain may play tricks on the memory.

Since all experience is believed to be recorded somewhere in the brain, the ability to recall is crucial to the memory process. The lack of that ability is like being unable to retrieve information from a filing system or from a computer. Memory is thought to be closely related to intelligence, but not all persons with excessive memories are of superior intelligence. On the contrary, some persons of below average intelligence have an incredible ability to remember data in specific limited areas. I knew a mentally handicapped man who, though he could not read or write and could not speak intelligibly, was able to identify the names and uniform numbers of hundreds of baseball players. Tom Fuller, "the Virginia Calculator," who was born in 1712 and came to this country from Africa as a slave when he was still a boy, could multiply mentally two numbers of nine figures each, though he was totally illiterate.

There are those, on the other hand, whose exceptional memory is due to superior mental endowment. I read about Friedreich Wolf, the German philosopher and critic, at the age of five could recall ten to fifteen lines of poetry after a single reading. By the age of twelve he had memorized two-thirds of an English dictionary, and later he memorized an entire Greek dictionary. Johann Gottlieb Fichte, another German philosopher, as a little boy could listen to a sermon by the village pastor and then repeat it from memory. Chateaubriand, the French author and statesman, could repeat a sermon word for word, even when he had not paid close attention to it! Would having such a person in the congregation be an asset or a liability to a preacher?

Such feats of memory are astonishing in view of the fact that psychologists tell us people of average intelligence forget about half of what they have heard immediately after hearing it, no matter how carefully they were listening. This could be a discouraging thought to preachers, who must reconcile themselves to the fact that much of what they say in the pulpit will be quickly forgotten by most of the congregation, not because they were not paying attention, but simply because that's the way the mind works.

How, then, can we justify the subtitle of this chapter? It would seem that we should be addressing our *inability* to remember, rather than our *freedom* to remember. Quite so, if this were an essay on the contemporary view of the memory process, which looks upon remembering as a function of the individual human mind. The biblical concept of remembering, however, is entirely different. To the Hebrew remembering was not so much an individual as a communal matter. The community was the custodian of the corporate memory, which in the earliest days was passed on by oral tradition.

One cannot read the Old Testament without realizing the tremendous role of memory in the faith and life of Israel. The people were continually being exhorted to remember what God had done for them. "Thou shalt remember the LORD thy God.... Remember the days of old.... Remember the Sabbath day.... Remember his marvelous works...." Israel's faith was rooted in the remembrance of God's mighty acts. Yahweh had delivered them out of bondage in Egypt; therefore they must obey his commandments and keep his statutes.

On the individual level memory was closely associated with the perpetuating of a name. To remember a name was in effect to keep a person's name alive. This is why the Jewish patriarchal society attached such great significance to the birth of a son and to the giving of names. If a man had no sons, he could still keep his name alive by setting up a memorial, as did Absalom, who said, "'I have no son to keep my name in remembrance'; he called the pillar by his own name. It is called Absalom's Monument to this day" (2 Samuel 18:18). The worst thing that could happen was for a man's name to be blotted out. Thus the Israelites called upon Yahweh to blot out the names of their enemies.

The biblical concept of remembering differed from the modern view, furthermore, in that it was more than a mere mental process. To remember God's commandments was to obey them. To remember the Sabbath day was to keep it holy. To remember God's mercies was to give God thanks and praise. Thus remembering implied a response, and it was practically synonymous with the action it called forth. We see that especially when the verb is used with God as the subject, which is most frequently the case in the

Old Testament. In remembering, God shows mercy, or judges, or delivers, or protects, or punishes.

When in the New Testament, therefore, Paul exhorted Timothy to remember Jesus Christ, he was not suggesting a mental exercise. He was not inviting Timothy to engage in some sentimental reflection, a dreamy nostalgia, a pillow picture, such as the poet Thomas Moore wrote about:

> *Oft in the stilly night, ere slumber's chain has bound me,*
> *fond memory brings the light of other days around me;*
> *the smiles, the tears, of boyhood's years,*
> *the words of love then spoken;*
> *The eyes that shone now dimmed and gone,*
> *the cheerful hearts now broken.*[52]

This was not Paul's idea of remembering Christ. Paul was a Jew and his use of the verb carried with it all the rich meaning of the Hebrew. He had just finished urging Timothy to be strong and to take his share of the suffering as a good soldier of Christ. No soldier gets involved in civilian pursuits, wrote Paul, since the soldier's aim is to satisfy the enlisting officer. Nor is an athlete crowned unless he or she competes according to the rules. And it is the hard-working farmer who gets the first share of the crops (II Timothy 2:3-6).

These three metaphors all teach the same lesson: Christians must give themselves wholeheartedly to their role as disciples, exercising discipline and self-control at all times. "Think over what I say," wrote Paul, "for the Lord will give you understanding in all things" (II Timothy 2:7). That is, the Holy Spirit will enable you to apply these lessons to your own life. Then, following this advice, Paul went on to say, "Remember Jesus Christ raised from the dead, a descendant of David — that is my gospel" (v. 8). If he were actually talking to Timothy, he probably would be saying something like this:

> *Yes, Timothy, in your suffering, remember Christ, who felt the Roman lash and bore the cross and died on Calvary alone and accursed, though he had committed no*

122

wrong. It is he who bids us "Follow!" and the path he trod was a path of suffering. But mine is not a gospel of suffering, Timothy. It would be a morbid story indeed, if it ended there, a sinless man nailed to a cross. What joy and hope could such an ending have for us? Remember Jesus Christ raised from the dead! — Christ who through suffering triumphed over tragedy, Christ the eternal Son of God, Christ raised from the dead! Herein lies our hope, Timothy — the resurrection of Christ, the supreme demonstration of God's love, the final proof of Jesus' claim to be the Savior of the world.

Remember Jesus Christ, raised from the dead — and a descendant of David! Yes, he was truly divine, but he was also fully human. He was a man of flesh and blood, descended from David as the Scriptures foretold. He was no apparition, no divine phantom. He ate and drank and worked and played and laughed and cried like any other human being. He felt the pangs of thirst and pain and sorrow and loneliness and temptation. Yet God was in this man, reconciling the world to himself, this man descended from David.

This is my gospel, Timothy, the gospel you have always heard me preach and teach, the gospel for which I am suffering and wearing fetters like a criminal right now. But the word of God is not fettered, and so I endure everything for the sake of those who believe in Christ, that they may obtain salvation. So remember Jesus Christ, raised from the dead, a descendant of David — that is my gospel!

Such was the meaning behind Paul's words to Timothy, words which could well have been spoken to us today. We, too, have the freedom to remember Jesus Christ, raised from the dead, and the freedom to enjoy the strength and comfort that freedom brings. For these words are intended to be a source of encouragement and hope to all who would be soldiers of Christ. To remember Jesus is not just a duty, it is a blessed privilege. For to remember him as the Bible uses that term is to feel the power, the strength, the comfort, the hope of knowing a living Lord and Savior.

Because we remember Jesus, we are free to remember our past. We don't have to blot out our mistakes, our blunders, our sins, because Christ has done that for us already. Remembering thus is a redemptive process; instead of trying to hide or deny our mistakes, we can allow our mistakes to be the catalysts for transformation and renewal. Instead of stumbling blocks, they become stepping stones to a new life. This is the beauty of the Alcoholics Anonymous program, whose members begin their testimony by declaring, "I am an alcoholic."

In my work with prison inmates over the years I have found that they respond to this aspect of the gospel. Instead of denying their guilt in the typical manner, they discover the possibility of a reclaimed life in the knowledge that God loves them and accepts them as they are, if they confess their sins and are truly sorry for their mistakes. Because they are free to remember, they are free to confess and to be redeemed.

Chuck Colson, of Watergate fame, is a wonderful example. So was a less well known man named Bill, who claimed to be an atheist, when I first visited him in prison. He was discouraged and embittered, but in time he repented, accepted Christ, and dedicated his life to telling others about a God who can help us overcome our mistakes and change our lives. He was eventually released and was taken under care of a church. He applied and was admitted to a theological seminary, graduated three years later, was ordained, and became the pastor of a church and director of a Halfway House, helping to rehabilitate ex-convicts back into society.

What is true for prison inmates is no less true for you and me, if we, too, remember our sins and the Christ who died that we might be forgiven. What a privilege it is to be free to remember! Why, then, do so many people not avail ourselves of that freedom? How slow some are to remember the one who was raised from the dead, when they become weighted down by past mistakes, or the problems of life, or the pressures of work, or whatever. "Come to me, all you that are weary and are carrying heavy burdens, and I will give you rest," said Jesus (Matthew 11:28). "O what peace we often forfeit, O what needless pain we bear, all because we do not carry everything to God in prayer." I repeat: What a friend we have in Jesus!

Why don't we remember Christ? Could it be that unconscious will to forget, that psychologists talk about? Or could it be a fear that the gospel may not be true, or an unwillingness to accept its demands upon us, if it is true? Or could it be a moral arrogance that knows no need of a Savior? Or an intellectual snobbishness that can't conceive of a risen Christ? Is it procrastination? Or apathy? Or ignorance? Or a stubborn unwillingness to take the leap of faith?

Why don't we remember Christ? Perhaps it's the penalty of being human, the peril of reason. Maybe it's the price of free will. No one can make himself or herself believe in Jesus, let alone force anyone else to believe. You can't win someone to Christ by argument, nor can you disprove Christ to someone who wants to believe.

"I know that my Redeemer lives!" exclaimed Job (19:25), and so do millions and millions of Christians throughout the world today. They know it. They can't prove it, but they know it. He lives! They know it because his Spirit dwells in them, and testifies in their hearts that what the Bible says about him is true.

If the essence of our humanity is our superior ability to remember, then the essence of our Christianity is our willingness to remember Christ. In him we are free to remember who we are, because we remember whose we are.

When to the cross I turn mine eyes,
and rest on Calvary,
O Lamb of God, my Sacrifice,
I must remember thee.

Remember thee, and all thy pains,
and all thy love to me,
yea, while a breath, a pulse remains,
will I remember thee.

And when these failing lips grow dumb,
and mind and memory flee,
when thou shalt in thy kingdom come,
Jesus remember me.[53]

Questions For Personal Reflection And/Or Group Discussion

1. What kinds of things do you remember from your childhood? Draw a picture that represents your very earliest memory.

2. What do you want those who come after you to remember about you?

3. Are things in your past which you don't want to remember? Why don't you want to remember those things?

4. Why does the Bible place so much emphasis on remembering? What kinds of things does God want us to remember?

5. How does faith in Christ free us to remember? What are the benefits of that freedom?

6. What does it mean to remember Christ? When and how do we do that?

Chapter Thirteen

Forget About It!
Free To Forget

Remembering and forgetting are so closely related that it is difficult to consider one without the other. We forget things we ought to remember, and we remember things we ought to forget. It is helpful, nevertheless, to consider each of these topics separately in the context of our call to freedom in Jesus Christ, since they are different in one obvious sense: It is much more difficult to remember than it is to forget! We wish we could remember more and forget less.

Our problem, it would seem, is one of remembering, not forgetting. Forgetting comes easily enough; we don't have to work at it. We forget much of what we learned in school; we forget the names of people we've met; we forget things we meant to say or do; we forget faces, facts, and figures we wish we could recall at will; we forget all sorts of things we don't want to forget. Would that we all, like the Amazing Kreskin, could read and remember the contents of a book in twenty minutes.

But just as there are some things we ought to remember, so too there are things that we *ought* to forget, that we are *free* to forget in Jesus Christ. Here I am using the word to mean not a lapse of memory but a conscious mental avoidance. We are free to forget in the sense of not lingering on a past occurrence. Many who call themselves Christians have never understood that freedom. They torture themselves with the memory of things they need not or should not remember. In spite of what appears to be an unlimited capacity for forgetting, they don't seem to want to forget the things they ought to forget, the things which God has given us the freedom to forget.

What are these things? There are three main kinds or categories. First, there are the evils which befall us, for which no one is responsible. Death robs us of someone we love; our home is struck by lightning and destroyed by fire; an automobile accident leaves us permanently disabled. Tragedies like these can and do happen to many of us. They are hard to take, of course. We suffer for a time, of course. But to dwell too long on such a calamity is not healthful or helpful. We must let time heal the wounds of the spirit.

I'm not suggesting that we never think about a loved one who has died. I don't want to forget my parents, or my brother, or the son my wife and I lost, or any of our deceased friends and loved ones. But to dwell too much on past sorrows is morbid. "The Moving Finger writes," said Omar Khayyam, "and having writ moves on. Nor all thy piety nor wit shall lure it back to cancel half a line, nor all thy tears wash out a word of it."[54]

Why can't we forget our sorrows? Probably because we haven't let God help us forget them. We haven't taken them to the Lord in prayer. To quote once again a line from one of my favorite hymns, "O what peace we often forfeit! O what needless pain we bear, all because we do not carry, everything to God in prayer."[55] And it's not enough to take our trouble to God; we have to learn to leave it there, and forget it.

The evils that befall us are the first thing we ought to forget. Our past successes and failures are the second. With regard to our successes, we are free in Christ not to dwell on our past accomplishments but always to be striving forward toward a higher goal, the prize of our high calling in Christ. It is not our past successes but our present service that counts with God. In Christ we are freed from the necessity of constantly reminding ourselves and others about the great things we have done. Instead we can rejoice in the great things God has done and will do for, with, and through those who are seeking to know and to do God's will.

Forgetting our past failures is more complicated and hence more challenging than forgetting our successes. Most of us have failed at least once in our lives, failed to achieve some goal we sought, some prize we desired, some standard of performance we hoped to attain. All of us have made mistakes and done things for which we are sorry, especially when our mistakes have been costly.

A certain amount of regret over past failures is not only natural but necessary and proper. A conscientious person will surely be sorry for his or her mistakes. But too often we let these things get us down. We worry too much about things we've said and done. We dwell so much on our past ineffectiveness that our present effectiveness is impaired.

But that's not what Paul said we who are mature in our faith ought to do. "This one thing I do," he told the Philippians, "forgetting what lies behind and straining forward to what lies ahead, I press on toward the goal for the prize of the heavenly call of God in Christ Jesus" (3:13b-14). Paul's advice is, If we can't do anything about what lies behind, forget it. If we can do something to correct our mistakes, then by all means let's do it. But let's not worry about things over which we have no control. Don't cry over spilt milk; wipe it up!

Paul's rule holds true whether our past failures are innocent mistakes or sinful mistakes. The two are obviously different in kind. Some of our mistakes are not morally wrong. They are merely the result of poor judgment, or lack of ability, or misguided enthusiasm. Most of us would agree that we have a right to forget this kind of mistake. Here it is just a matter of being willing to accept the consequences of our mistakes. For example, we make a poor investment and it costs us some money. There's nothing to do but accept the loss and try to do better the next time.

But when it comes to those mistakes we call sins, it's a different story. Here we have to deal with that troublesome thing called the conscience, and forgetting comes a lot harder. It is at this point especially that we Christians must be reminded of our freedom to forget, our right to forget the sins which God has already forgiven. This is the wonderful thing about the Christian faith: it's not what we have been, but what we now are that counts with God. God is interested in our present, not our past. Oh, we'll pay for our sins, one way or another; sooner or later we'll suffer the consequences of our misdeeds. But that suffering can be a stepping stone to a deeper faith. We could not find a better example than Paul himself, who had much to forget. Before his conversion he had been a persecutor of the Christians. He had Stephen's death on his conscience and the imprisonment of countless others. But he didn't let that stop him from accepting the call of God. He didn't refuse the call because of his past mistakes; he didn't decline because he felt unworthy. Not at all, he forgot the past, gave his heart to Christ, and became the greatest apostle of the one whose followers he had formerly persecuted.

Why can't we be like Paul? Why can't we forget our mistakes? Is it because we don't have enough faith? I think many of us haven't really learned to forgive ourselves, because we haven't accepted God's forgiveness. We haven't accepted the promise of the gospel, the promise that Christ died for our sins. We say the words, but do we really believe them? Do we know what it means to say Christ died for our sins? If we do, then we should be able to forget them.

If I may be very personal at this point, I must confess that this is one of the most difficult things for me. I have trouble forgetting my past mistakes, and that means I have not really accepted the fact that I am forgiven. I know it theologically and intellectually, but I worry about the fact that I go on doing some of the things for which I have asked forgiveness. I ask God's forgiveness for losing my temper or for some mean thought or hasty word, knowing that it will happen again, and I wonder how God can put up with the likes of me.

I realize these spiritual gymnastics are really a test of my faith. If Jesus told his disciples there is no limit to the number of times they should be willing to forgive a person (Matthew 18:21-22), is not God able to forgive us infinitely more? In other words, would Jesus expect us to be more forgiving than God? That is always the comforting thought that keeps me going, although the tension between forgetting and remembering my sins, between feeling guilty and knowing I am forgiven, is always there.

To those who can identify with my struggle, I hasten to add that a certain amount of guilt is healthful, but not when it reflects a lack of faith. How guilty should we feel? I would say guilty enough to make us truly sorry for whatever we've done, guilty enough to make us repent. And the moment we do repent and ask God's forgiveness is the moment we are forgiven and are free to forget.

We also know that it is not enough just to be sorry. We must correct our mistakes whenever we can. We must set right whatever wrongs we can, and make restitution wherever possible. Until we've done this, we'll never be free to forget, because our sin will be on our conscience. It will be a present sin, not a past sin, and we can't forget the sins of the present because they are still with us.

If, then, we would make proper use of our freedom to forget, we need to learn to forget the evils that befall us through no fault of our own, as well as our own failures, whether they be honest mistakes or sinful misdeeds. And third, we need to forget the failures of others, again whether they be honest mistakes or outright sins. That does not mean we can't feel righteous indignation, whenever we encounter sin, or that we can't be critical of those who engage in it, so long as we don't assume a self-righteous attitude about it. But it does mean that we should not bear a grudge against someone for some injury or hurt he or she has caused us. We must learn to forget the insults and humiliation we receive from others.

This is not easy! It means we have to swallow our pride. It's hard to resist the temptation to justify oneself. It's hard enough to keep from striking back; it's harder still to keep from harboring resentment within. Humiliation is a cross we don't bear easily. We'd rather bear a grudge than a cross.

But Paul's advice still holds true. We've got to learn to forget these things, or else we'll be like those sour individuals we often meet, who are critical of everything and everybody, because they can't forget what someone has done to them, or more likely, what they *imagine* has been done to them. This is not good. One of the worst sins of all is the sin of refusing to be reconciled. Those who refuse to make up after a quarrel are sinning not only against their brother or sister, but against God! Jesus expects us to be reconciled to one another (Matthew 5:24).

With apologies to the late Pearl Bailey for doctoring a line from a song she made popular many years ago, "It takes two to tangle!" It takes two to make an argument, but it takes only one to keep it going. Christians are not free to engage in arguments about "who struck John?" Whatever happened is water under the bridge. We can't make up with someone by trying to rehash old arguments; we end up where we began. The best rule is, Forget it! It's what we want the relationship to be *now* that counts, not what it used to be. There must be a willingness on both sides to give and take, to say I'm sorry, and mean it.

If we could only realize this, how much better off the world would be! Relationships among relatives, friends, neighbors, business associates, would be much more harmonious. What a difference it could make in labor-management relations, international peace negotiations, trade agreements, wherever people meet under adversarial conditions. In the home, the school, the church, the community, the nation, the world, people would get along so much better, if they would learn to forget past grievances and concentrate on improving their present relationships.

Why don't people do this? Our sinful pride, for one thing — the need to be right, the need to be vindicated. No one likes to be humiliated. Then there is that subtle, human desire for revenge, which takes a sadistic pleasure in putting the other person down, telling somebody off, getting even.

Perhaps there is also an element of self-pity involved; some people like to feel sorry for themselves, so they go on nursing their wounds and bearing their grudges. As long as they can convince themselves they have a legitimate gripe, they can go on criticizing others and inflate their own ego in the process. Some people think the way to build themselves up is to tear other people down.

All of these reasons reflect a lack of love, without which we can never learn to forget the hurts we receive from others. If we really have the love of Christ in us, we can't hate our brother or sister. "Those who say 'I love God' and hate their brothers or sisters are liars" (I John 4:20a). If we can love, we can forget.

The question remains, of course, How? How does one learn to forget the meanness of other people? You just can't make yourself love someone you dislike with a snap of your fingers. You can't make yourself overlook a wrong just by saying, "Forget it!" That's like trying to lift yourself up by your own bootstraps, and the bootstrap method simply won't work. We need God's help. As I have already said, it is a matter of faith, and faith itself is a gift of God.

It's only in the context of faith that we can speak of our freedom to forget. That's where our freedom to forget and our freedom to remember are joined, for to forget our sins we must remember God's forgiveness. To forget another's wrongs, we must remember God's love. To forget sorrows or hurts of any kind, we must remember our calling in Christ, forgetting what lies behind and straining forward to what lies ahead. Paul didn't forget the past by shutting his eyes, and pretending it didn't happen. He knew what was behind him, but he kept his face forward. No one can run a good race while looking back over the shoulder, and that's not the way Paul ran the race of life. He was always pressing on toward the goal, like Jesus, who kept his face steadfast toward Jerusalem.

In other words, if we are to forget something, we're going to have to substitute a worthier object for our attention. The best way to forget your own troubles is to help others bear theirs. The best way to forget a hurt is to help the person who hurt you. We don't help ourselves to forget by repaying an injury in kind, or returning insult for insult. We haven't truly forgotten until we can repay injury not in kind, but with kindness. That's what Jesus meant by turning the other cheek (Matthew 5:39; Luke 6:29). Forgetting must involve some positive action.

Again, the relation between forgiving and forgetting is crucial.

> *Among my other sins, I hope the Lord's forgiveness will*
> *include my failure to forgive,when I am angry still.*
> *There is another problem, though: Have I forgiven yet,*
> *if I say "I forgive" but in my heart I don't forget?*[56]

We can say "I forgive you," but have we really forgiven the person if we have not forgotten the wrong? If the old animus keeps rearing its ugly head, long after we thought we had forgiven the offense, have we really forgiven the offender? It is true that things can pop into our heads long after the fact, long after we thought we had erased them from our mind. That kind of spontaneous, unexpected recollection cannot be avoided, but it can be ignored. That is to say, we do not have to rehearse the former grievance and so revive our enmity. Rather we can once again pray for God to give us a spirit

133

of forgiveness and rid us of any lingering resentment. Human nature being what it is, forgiving and forgetting are an on-going process.

The freedom to forget begins not with our willingness to forgive, however, but with the recognition of our own need for forgiveness. It's not enough to say "I forgive you." I must begin by saying "Forgive me!" Sometimes what we're really saying when we say "I forgive you," is "I'm right and you're wrong, but I'll be big about it and forgive you." There can never be real reconciliation until both parties are willing to say, "Forgive me," as well as "I forgive you." Forgiving and asking forgiveness go hand in hand. You can't have one without the other.

I had thought of subtitling this chapter "Free to Forgive," but the importance of forgetting in that process, and its intricate correlation with the process of remembering convinced me that a chapter on our freedom to remember should be followed logically by a chapter on our freedom to forget, so that these two opposite but related aspects of Christian behavior could be dealt with separately but sequentially. There is much more to be said on both subjects, but I hope they have been covered sufficiently in relation to the theme of this book.

To illustrate the connection between our being free to remember and free to forget, and their dual relation to the theme of forgiveness, I want to conclude this chapter with a brief story. My cousin Amy has worked as a missionary for the Wycliffe Bible Translators ever since she graduated from nursing school. I remember how distressed she was by a tragedy involving some of her colleagues in that worthy organization.

Five young missionaries, Nate Saint, Jim Elliot, Roger Youderian, Ed McCully, and Peter Fleming, were trying to establish contact with the Auca tribe, more properly known as the Huaorani, deep in the Ecuadorian jungle. The word Auca in the Quechua language means "savage." The Americans had found a sandbar where they could land their small airplane, and during several flights into the jungle they had exchanged greetings and gifts with members of the tribe. They knew of the tribe's violent ways, and had vowed among themselves that they would not defend themselves against human attack. All seemed to be going well, when on

January 8, 1956, the project ended very tragically. The five men were speared to death by a group of the people they had come to help. It seemed such a cruel and unjust end to their mission of good will.

And what a terrible shock to their families! Can we imagine the anguish, the despair, the emptiness, the bitterness they must have felt? Could we blame the wives of those men if they had felt that their husbands' lives had been sacrificed for nothing, and that their own lives were meaningless and empty?

That was not their attitude at all. Three years later Rachel Saint, Nate's sister, and Elizabeth Elliot, Jim's widow, went to live with the very tribe who had committed the murders, so that the work for Christ could go on! Here was an example of forgiveness and love that amazed and eventually won even those savage minds.[57]

When I think of the petty things we let disturb us, the trivial slights that upset us so much and separate us from one another, I am moved once again to affirm that God in Christ has given us the freedom to forget the things we need to forget! May we, like Paul, press on toward the goal of the prize of the heavenly call of God in Christ Jesus — the call to freedom!

Awake, my soul, stretch every nerve, and press with vigor on,
a heavenly race demands thy zeal, and an immortal crown.
A cloud of witnesses around hold thee in full survey.
Forget the steps already trod, and onward urge thy way.[58]

Questions For Personal Reflection
And/Or Group Discussion

1. Are there things beyond your control in your past that you think about more than you should? Make a list of things you should "let go of."

2. Are you able to *forget* as well as forgive wrongs done to you, when people apologize for what they've done? What if they don't apologize?

3. Are you able to forgive yourself for mistakes you have made? Do you believe God forgives you, even when you repeat your mistakes?

4. Are your carrying any grudges or harboring any resentment toward anyone? Are you willing to take the initiative in seeking to be reconciled to the person or persons?

5. How does or should your faith in Christ free you to forget the wrongs done to you?

6. How would you explain to someone else the relation between these two aspects of Christian freedom, our freedom to remember and our freedom to forget?

Chapter Fourteen

A Reason To Be Proud
Free To Be Proud

According to the Bible and our Christian faith the essence of sin is pride. It is human beings' declaring themselves to be independent of God, arrogating unto themselves the glory that is due God alone. This was Adam's sin, and as humanity's representative, he stands for all of us. One poet philosopher put it this way:

> *In pride, in reasoning pride, our error lies;*
> *all quit their sphere, and rush into the skies.*
> *Pride still is aiming at the blest abodes:*
> *Men would be angels, angels would be gods.*[59]

"According to Christian teachers," wrote C. S. Lewis, "the essential vice, the utmost evil, is Pride. Unchastity, anger, greed, drunkenness, and all that, are mere flea-bites in comparison. It was through Pride that the devil became the devil. Pride leads to every other vice; it is the complete anti-God state of mind."[60]

If what C. S. Lewis said is true, how are we to understand the apostle Paul, when he confidently claims, "In Christ Jesus, then, I have reason to be proud of my work for God" (Romans 15:17)? Is Paul guilty of the basic human sin? Yes, and no. Yes, because Paul, like every other human being who ever lived, had his share of pride. He wasn't perfect, as he himself emphatically declared. He was a sinner standing in the need of prayer and God's forgiveness, like everyone else. He even referred to himself "the foremost of sinners" (I Timothy 1:15).

Yes, he was guilty of the basic human sin of pride, but not in this instance. In the first place, he was not claiming credit for himself. He said *"In Christ Jesus* I have reason to be proud," not in himself, but in Christ. Everything Paul did, everything he said, everything he was, he did and said and was by the grace of God. "By the grace of God, I am what I am," he told the Corinthians (I Corinthians 15:10), and to the Galatians he wrote, "It is no longer I who live, but it is Christ who lives in me.... May I never boast of anything except the cross of our Lord Jesus Christ..." (2:20, 6:14).

In Christ Jesus, then, Paul had reason to be proud of his work for God — *of his work for God*! That was the second modifying condition of Paul's pride. On the human level he had much to boast about. He made this point many times, most impressively in his second letter to the church at Corinth:

> *... Whatever anyone dares to boast of — I am speaking as a fool — I also dare to boast of that. Are they Hebrews? So am I. Are they Israelites? So am I. Are they descendants of Abraham? So am I. Are they ministers of Christ? I am talking like a madman — I am a better one: with far greater labors, far more imprisonments, with countless floggings, and often near death. Five times I have received from the Jews the forty lashes minus one. Three times I was beaten with rods. Once I received a stoning. Three times I was shipwrecked; for a night and a day I was adrift at sea; on frequent journeys, in danger from rivers, danger from bandits, danger from my own people, danger from Gentiles, danger in the city, danger in the wilderness, danger at sea, danger from false brothers and sisters, in toil and hardship, through many a sleepless night, hungry and thirsty, often without food, cold and naked...* (II Corinthians 11:21-28).

Who could have suffered more for Christ than Paul? He did indeed have much of which to be proud, but he said, "If I must boast, I will boast of the things that show my weakness" (II Corinthians 11:30-32). Paul's pride was in his work for God. He was pleased by the progress which the Roman Christians had made, and because he had been called by God's grace to be a minister of Christ to the Gentiles, so that their faith might be acceptable to God, Paul was proud of his work for God. "For I will not venture to speak of anything except what Christ has accomplished through me to win obedience from the Gentiles by word and deed" (Romans 15:18).

There must be, then, a kind of pride that is not altogether sinful, the kind of pride that Paul had, and the Psalmist when he cried, "My soul makes its boast in the LORD; let the humble hear and be glad" (Psalm 34:2). Knowing that many would deny that a Christian should ever feel any kind of pride, I felt the need to wrestle with the topic in this study of the implications of Christian freedom. In condemning all the ugly aspects of sinful pride, some people overlook what might even be called the virtues of pride. Perhaps benefits would be a better word.

Now, this is a very dangerous thought, so a word of caution is in order. We are dealing with a subtle paradox, and it is in no wise my intention to provide a convenient excuse for indulging our innate human weakness. In the light of what was said about pride in the preceding chapter, this is by no means a justification of the sin of pride. It is rather an attempt to understand how a person might have, as Paul had, a godly "reason to be proud."

In Christ Jesus we, too, can have reason to be proud of our work for God. Accepting the fact that whatever we may accomplish is solely by the grace of God working in us, we can feel the same kind of pride that Paul felt, an outgoing pride that has as its object not oneself, but Jesus Christ. The paradox is that only a humble person can experience this kind of pride; only a person whose strength is in God can say with Paul, "Such is the confidence that we have through Christ toward God. Not that we are competent of ourselves to claim anything as coming from us; our competence is from God" (2 Corinthians 3:4-5).

Again, the danger is evident, for even this pride is a sweet syrup that soon spoils, a vulnerable quality most susceptible to contamination and pollution. In one of his classic works, Reinhold Niebuhr discussed three kinds of pride: pride of power, pride of knowledge, and pride of virtue. The last, he said, makes virtue the very vehicle of sin and issues forth in spiritual pride, which is the ultimate of self-righteousness and self-deification. There is no final guarantee against spiritual pride, said Niebuhr. Even the recognition that one is a sinner can be a source of pride.[61]

A pride there is of rank — a pride of birth,
a pride of learning, and a pride of purse,
a London pride —in short, there be on earth
a host of prides, some better and some worse;
but of all prides, since Lucifer's attaint,
the proudest swells a self-elected saint[62]

Recognizing, therefore, the dangers to which we are all susceptible in these various forms of pride, in what way does our call to freedom in Christ allow us to be proud? *We are free to be proud when our pride is an incentive to fulfill our calling to serve God and our fellow human beings.* Pride can be a worthy incentive. No one knows this better than a preacher, every time he or she faces the awesome responsibility of expounding the word of God. Without an element of pride a preacher could be less conscientious about the task, even slovenly or slothful. Pride makes us want to do our best, not for our own sake, but for God's sake and for the sake of the congregations to whom we preach.

I have wrestled with this aspect of pride ever since I became a minister. In my prayers I have continually asked God to give me the right kind of pride, just enough to make me do my very best for God but not so much that I forget to give God all the glory, honor, and praise for whatever positive response I may receive. I ask God to forgive me if I am consciously or unconsciously seeking the praise of others instead of striving to please God.

Pride can be an incentive for anyone in whatever worthy endeavor she or he may undertake for God. We glorify God by using to the fullest extent the gifts God has given us. So whatever your occupation, make it a Christian vocation (calling) by being a Christian on the job, serving Christ on and off the job, for God's sake, not to build up your own ego but to honor God, who gives you the potential to be what you are. We are free to be proud when our pride is an incentive for noble effort.

We are also free to be proud when it's an expression of selfless devotion. It is a strange parent who does not take any pride in the achievements of his or her child. Pity the daughter or son who has no pride in her or his parents. Pity the parents! There are degrees, of course, to this kind of pride, too, but surely there is room for a certain amount of pride as a mark of affection. It is the kind of pride which Christ elicited from his heavenly Father, who declared, "This is my Son, the Beloved, with whom I am well pleased" (Matthew 3:17).

Yet we must be aware of the dangers here, too, for often the affectionate pride of parents can blind them to the faults of their children, as any teacher knows, and children can be sadly disillusioned or disappointed when their balloon of innocent adulation for a parent is punctured.

I shall never forget how chagrined our then four-year old son Woody was when he discovered that his father was not the biggest and strongest man in the world. "Lots of people are bigger than you, Daddy," he sobbed mournfully. For the rest of the day he was glum, but when I tucked him into bed that night, he brightened up. "That's all right, Daddy," he commented, as if suddenly consoled by a new thought, "at least you're bigger than Miss Cadell." She was the diminutive church secretary, a 72-year old bundle of energy in a 5-foot frame.

The right kind of pride will help us to be pleased about the right kinds of things in our loved ones. That means not just their winning games, getting good marks, earning raises, landing promotions, getting elected, and similar achievements, admirable as these things might be, but pride in the good that is in them as persons, pride in whatever is kind and compassionate and brave and loyal and true, whatever is Christlike. We need to help our children, especially, to understand what it is we value the most about them — not just the level of their achievements but the quality of their lives.

It's true for adults as well; it's not one's position in the world but the integrity of one's character that matters most, as Paul reminded the Christians at Corinth. "We are not commending ourselves to you again but giving you cause to be proud of us, so that you may be able to answer those who pride themselves on one's position and not on one's heart" (II Corinthians 5:12).

As parents, moreover, our pride should not be in ourselves, as if we were responsible for these qualities in our children. We must know ourselves to be only the instruments that God has used, and we must constantly throw ourselves upon God's grace and mercy, when our children leave the nest.

Pride as incentive, pride as devotion, and then there is *pride as power.* The right kind of pride can enable you to keep your head up, when you are otherwise down and out. It's not power over others, but the power to be a better person, the power to overcome adversity, to live with pain, to keep going when you feel like quitting. This kind of pride is akin to dignity and self-respect. It is not expressed by haughty superiority, or snobbish arrogance, or false modesty, nor is it the kind of pride that refuses to accept help when it is offered in good faith.

The pride of power is the pride that enables us to bear the cross, to keep our chin up, to say with Paul, "I can do all things through him who strengthens me" (Philippians 4:13). Such pride is beautiful to behold. It is the pride of the martyrs who counted it a privilege to suffer for Christ. They were free to be proud to live and die for their Lord and Savior.

And we are free to feel the kind of pride that comes with the knowledge that one has been used by God. It is *pride as reward,* the kind of pride Paul was expressing, when he declared, "In Christ Jesus, then, I have reason to be proud of my work for God." This kind of pride is not a form of smugness, or complacency, or self-justification. Nor is it always a predictable feeling. It seems rather to come over you when you least expect it. God has a way of buoying up our spirits, when we need it, by revealing to us some evidence of spiritual growth, or moral accomplishment, which is God's way of letting us know that our efforts never go unnoticed by God. For God can turn even our failures into victories, as long as we are willing to forget ourselves and let God take over. This kind of pride rests not in oneself, but in God. It is an unseen pat on the back which God gives those with whom God is well pleased. One can never confer it upon oneself.

Pride as reward is very closely related to *pride as exaltation.* The psalmist was a good example of this aspect of pride, when he declared, "Some take pride in chariots, and some in horses, but our pride is in the name of the LORD our God" (Psalm 20:7). Paul, again, was another worthy example. His pride was a joyful affirmation of the unspeakable riches of Christ. He gloried not in himself but in Christ. The fact of his conversion, the fact that Christ could transform him from a persecutor of the church into a dynamic apostle for Christ, the fact that God was using him to bear witness to the Gentile world, the fact that through his preaching and teaching many were being won to Christ — all of these incredible realities were a source of immense joy to Paul. He exalted in the wisdom, power, and grace of God.

Power, **R**eward, **I**ncentive, **D**evotion, **E**xaltation — arranged in that order they form an acrostic that spells **PRIDE**, the kind of pride we who have been called to freedom have a right to feel, even though it is never devoid of the element of sin. It is the kind of pride we should pray for, the kind that stirs us to higher purpose and worthier effort, the kind that springs not from one's own achievements but from one's relationship to Christ. For it is only through Christ that human pride can be anything other than the base sin it usually is. For freedom Christ has set us free to be proud of our work for God, as Paul was.

Paul's work for God was to be a missionary to the Gentiles. He was a tentmaker by trade, but his pride was in his work for God. This is where our pride should be. The right to work for God is ours. We have been called to be Christ's servants and his witnesses. Those who give themselves wholeheartedly to that task, whatever their stage of life, whatever their circumstances, sooner or later may well feel the kind of pride Paul felt, the pride of those who have seen the work of God in and through themselves, pride not in their own ability, but in the Savior they love.

You may be thinking, what can I do for God? If nothing else, you can share your faith with others. You can tell others what God has done for you lately. You can show them by the way you speak and act that you "serve a risen Savior, who is in the world today."[63] When you experience the joy of sharing the good news of Christ with someone else, you will be able to say with Paul, "In Christ Jesus I have reason to be proud of my work for God."

How amazing it is that our call to freedom in Christ includes even the freedom to be proud! May it always be the right kind of pride!

There's a certain kind of pride that is okay.
It's a pride we seldom hear about today,
not an ego-centric pride
that is too preoccupied
with one's own achievements and what others say.

It's the pride of those who glory in the Lord,
those whose faithful service is its own reward,
those who are the first to know
where the credit has to go,
for they can do little of their own accord.

It's a pride reflecting grateful happiness
for the persons God has prompted to confess
faith in Jesus Christ the Son,
through whatever work they've done.
Only humble servants can such pride express.

What the Lord can do and has done is immense,
and the knowledge that we are God's instruments
in God's kingdom-building work,
if our task we do not shirk,
is a reason to be proud with reverence.[64]

Questions For Personal Reflection
And/Or Group Discussion

1. Do you know anyone who is overly prideful? Do you think that person is aware of it?

2. When you were a child, did you feel that your parent or parents were proud of you? At the time what kinds of things did you think made them proud of you?

3. Are there things about you of which you yourself are proud? Have you ever boasted or bragged about those things? How do you feel after you have done that?

4. Do you think there are legitimate kinds of pride? How would you describe them? What makes them proper? Have you ever observed these kinds of pride in someone else?

5. Can you think of examples from your own life of the five kinds of pride described in this chapter?

6. Could you tell someone how Christ frees believers to experience these kinds of pride?

Chapter Fifteen

Is Anybody Happy?
Free To Be Joyful

Devotees of the big band era would remember Ted Lewis and his familiar catch word, "Is everybody happy?" In 1943 he played himself in a movie by that title. With apologies to the fans of the former band leader, I'd like to ask, "Is *anybody* happy?" Is anybody *really* happy?

When you consider the misery we all must eventually experience in this life, the sickness, the sorrow, the frustrations and disappointments, the boredom and monotony that characterize so much of our existence, the constant strain on our mental, physical, and emotional resources, the financial worries, the irritations of societal living, not to mention the natural disasters, accidents, and jarring set-backs that strike like lightning bolts out of the blue, plus the depressing realities of world hunger, poverty, and disease, international terrorism, drug trafficking, organized crime, political corruption, economic exploitation, the abuse of the environment and the misuse and waste of the Earth's resources, racial and religious violence, warring nations and tribes — when you think of all there is to be *unhappy* about, you have to wonder how anyone could really be happy. G. K. Chesterton might well have been talking about today, when he said, "Everywhere there is speed, noise, confusion, but nowhere deep happiness and quiet hearts."[65]

But there must be such a thing as happiness, else why would there be so much talk about it? *Some* people are happy; at least they *say* they are. Who are these happy people? Who is "the most happy fella"? Is it the person who uses the right deodorant, or drinks the right beer, or buys the right automobile, as their advertisers would have us believe? Certainly there must be more to happiness than that! I hardly think it was a commercial product that Alexander Pope had in mind when he wrote,

> *O happiness! our being's end and aim!*
> *Good, pleasure, ease, content! Whate'er thy name:*
> *that something still which prompts th'eternal sigh,*
> *for which we bear to live, or dare to die.*[66]

Happiness, as we generally use the term, is obviously both relative and subjective. Some people are happy under circumstances which others would find unbearable. I remember back in my baseball days being asked to arrange for a few of our players to visit a children's hospital, when the Orioles were playing in Boston. A group of us went and visited several of the wards. The players talked with the children, signed autographs, and gave out photographs. We also had baseballs for the real fans, and one little fellow was beaming with delight as he received a ball. "Golly," he said, "I'm the luckiest kid in the whole world!" The luckiest kid in the whole world was paralyzed from the waist down.

True happiness, you see, is a state of mind, and like true freedom it is not necessarily dependent upon the external circumstances of one's life. Remember Richard Cory?

> *Whenever Richard Cory went down town,*
> *   we people on the pavement looked at him;*
> *he was a gentleman from sole to crown,*
> *   clean favored, and imperially slim.*
> *And he was always quietly arrayed,*
> *   and he was always human when he talked;*
> *but still he fluttered pulses when he said,*
> *   "Good morning," and he glittered when he walked.*
> *And he was rich — yes, richer than a king—*
> *   and admirably schooled in every grace;*
> *in fine, we thought that he was everything*
> *   to make us wish that we were in his place.*
> *So on we worked, and waited for the light,*

and went without the meat, and cursed the bread;
and Richard Cory, one calm summer night,
went home and put a bullet through his head.[67]

Richard Cory had everything but happiness. Some people, on the other hand, have nothing, and yet they seem to be happy. They can be poor, or disabled, or terminally ill, and still they have a happy spirit.

If happiness cannot be measured by material possessions or the state of one's health, how does one become happy? The Psalmist declared, "Happy are the people whose God is the LORD!" (Psalm 14:15b). God is the ultimate source of human happiness, and to be truly happy, one must be close to God. The Old Testament writers regarded happiness as the result of divine favor, and they measured it in terms of material blessings, long life, abundant crops, peace, and prosperity. This is the prayer expressed in the section of the Psalm from which the above verse is taken. It is a wish for healthy sons and daughters, full storehouses, big herds, and for the absence of distress, and in the closing verse, the writer says: "Happy are the people to whom such blessings fall; happy are the people whose God is the LORD!" Thus he views God as the source of all blessings, and the greatest blessing of all is to be numbered among the people of God.

To "Christianize" that text, it means that those who believe in and follow Jesus are surely numbered among the people of God. In Jesus Christ, therefore, we are free to be happy, but ours is not what the world calls happiness. I have already made the point that true happiness cannot be measured in material terms, and being the people of God in the Christian sense does not mean that worldly prosperity will follow automatically. What Jesus promised was anything but worldly happiness. "You will be hated by all because of my name," he told the disciples (Matthew 10:22). "If any want to become my followers," he said on another occasion, "let them deny themselves and take up their cross and follow me" (Matthew 16:24; Mark 8:34; cf. Luke 9:23). That hardly sounds like the happy life!

The difference between worldly happiness and Christian happiness is the difference between temporary euphoria and abiding joy. Christian joy abides whether one is temporarily happy or not. Christian joy is God-related happiness. Christian happiness is an aspect of Christian joy. To understand our freedom to be joyful, one must distinguish between a worldly view of happiness and the *Christian* understanding of happiness, which is used here as a synonym for joy.

For the best description of Christian happiness, as Jesus would have us understand it, we have only to look at the beginning of his Sermon on the Mount, the section we call "the Beatitudes" (Matthew 5:3-11). The very first word which Jesus spoke to the multitude that day, as they sat on the hillside beneath the blue Galilean sky, was a word which in English means "happy." "Happy are the poor in spirit," Jesus began, "for theirs is the kingdom of heaven" (Matthew 5:3). Most of our English translations have "blessed," instead of "happy," but the word "happy" is actually a better translation of the Greek text, for it indicates a consciousness as well as a condition. Happiness is not merely a passive state; it is not just a condition bestowed on someone by God. When one is truly happy, one feels it; one is aware of one's happiness.

And so the divine message which Jesus preached that day began with a declaration of happiness. But who did he say was happy? The poor in spirit, those who mourn, the meek, the pure in heart, the peacemakers, those who are persecuted for righteousness' sake. Happiness is a condition which belongs to those who have these qualities. They are the happy people of God.

And why are they happy? Because theirs is the kingdom of heaven, because they shall be comforted, they shall inherit the earth, they shall be satisfied, they shall obtain mercy, they shall see God, they shall be called children of God. This is the perfect happiness which God offers God's people. It is God's desire, God's purpose, that we have it. Surely we can say with the Psalmist, "Happy are the people whose God is the LORD!" (144:15b).

The Beatitudes clearly indicate that Christian happiness is not a matter of possessions. It is a state of being, which results from the qualities that Jesus mentions. The degree to which they are present is the degree to which happiness is attained. These qualities are not of the fame and fortune variety. Rather they are attributes of true

Christian humility and submissiveness. This is the happiness of Jesus Christ, the happiness of which the apostle Paul speaks in his letter to Timothy, when he refers to "the glorious gospel of the happy God" (I Timothy 1:11). It is the happiness of a God who rejoices in being our Redeemer.

Given this understanding of happiness, was there anyone happier than Jesus Christ? Jesus was meekness itself. His was a perfect humility, a perfect righteousness. He bore the burdens of the sinful world upon his shoulders and mourned for those who would not believe. Yet he was merciful and gave his life to atone for the sins of humanity.

Too often we think of Jesus only as a solemn individual, who went around with a sorrowful look on his face all the time. He was indeed a man of sorrow and acquainted with grief. There were times when his heart bled with sadness, moments of physical agony and mental anguish. Surely he conducted himself with all the dignity befitting one who was conscious of a divine mission. But Jesus must have had a most engaging personality. No spiritual "sad sack" could have attracted the crowds he did. He *had* to be a compelling speaker. He could not talk about joy and happiness, and be glum. Surely his expression, his voice, his whole countenance must have conveyed the mood of his words. Though he knew he must suffer and die, he was a happy man. He was the bearer of good news, the good news of salvation and the kingdom of God.

Should not this tell us something about our own happiness? The gospel which we proclaim is good news. That, of course, is what the word gospel means: good news! It is a reason for joy. Why are some Christians so glum about it? In Jesus Christ we have the freedom to be joyful, but many believers don't seem to know it. They say they're happy because it rained, or it didn't rain, or because they're going to the shore, or because they have a new car, or a new job, or something of the sort, but they aren't happy about what they ought to be happy about: that Jesus Christ died for their sins, and that in him they have eternal life. This is what really matters, the one lasting source of true happiness. It's the reason Christians can be joyful even in the midst of sorrow. All other happiness is merely temporary, here today, gone tomorrow. But the inner joy and peace which belong to the people of God can be forever.

This is true happiness, Christian joy, and if we have it, it will show. How? By our words, our actions, our moods. Others know when they meet a genuinely joyful spirit. We don't show that kind of happiness by wearing a perpetual grin on our face, like the Cheshire cat in *Alice in Wonderland*. Christian happiness does not mean we are never sad, or sorry, or sick at heart. There is plenty of room for tears. But truly happy people, joyful people, can smile in the midst of their tears. They know that behind the dark clouds of doubt and discouragement is the sunshine of God's love, waiting to flood their lives with new hope. They can navigate the winding river of life without foundering on the mud bank of despair. They can do this because in Jesus Christ they are called to freedom, and that freedom includes the freedom to be joyful. Happy are those whose God is the Lord, because they know what God is like — and it shows!

I have noticed that joyful people are blessed with a keener sensitivity than other people. They are more sympathetic, more compassionate, more sensitive to and understanding of the needs and concerns of others. They grieve with them, share their misery, take their burdens upon their own heart. Perpetually sad, somber, sullen people are less able to help others. No one wants to tell one's troubles to gloomy Gus, because gloomy Gus is too wrapped up in his own troubles to listen to anyone else. Joyful people find happiness in sharing the load, in bearing one another's burdens. They are happiest when they are helping someone else.

On the other hand, they do not show their joy by *glorying* in sorrow and trouble. Some people seem to enjoy wallowing in misery. They relish hearing another's tale of woe, so they can pass it on to someone else. The juicier the story, the better they like it, and if it isn't gory enough, they are quick to embellish it.

And then there are those who I suspect actually enjoy being sad. They are always worrying about things that might happen, or about things that did happen years ago. They want others to feel sorry for them, and if they don't get the sympathy they want, they feel hurt and neglected. But that's all right with them, too, because it's something else to be sad about. If they aren't worried, they worry about not having anything to worry about.

Joyful people are not like that. They don't want trouble for trouble's sake. They don't *want* to be sad, but when misfortune does occur, they accept it courageously and try to understand God's will for their lives. Christian joy is rooted in the conviction that in everything God works for good with those who love God and are called according to God's purpose.

Joy is the necessary sequence of our faith in God. It is much more than merely having a sense of humor. That is part of it, to be sure. Jesus had a sense of humor and he used it to good advantage. But joy is not measured by the audibility of the laugh or the visibility of the smile. The funny person is not necessarily the happy person. Behind the jolly facade may beat the bleeding heart of a Pagliacci. Christian joy is not feigned, nor forced, nor soon forgotten. It is not a fleeting breeze that cools a flaming temper for a time. It is the harmonious accompaniment of Christian character, which engulfs a person's whole being with the heavenly music of God's amazing grace.

One cannot keep such joy to oneself. Christian joy cannot be felt unless it is shared. When you see a good movie, you want to tell others about it. When you gaze upon a glorious sunset, you enjoy it more if someone else is there to watch it with you. "All who joy would win must share it," commented the poet Byron; "happiness was born a twin.[68] The spirit of Christ cannot be bottled up. The joy he brings must be shared.

So, what is there to be happy about? There is everything in the world to be happy about. For Jesus Christ *is* everything. As the song says, "He's everything to me." God sent the Son to show us the way to true happiness, and in him our happiness, our joy, is complete. He has made us heirs of the kingdom of God. It is not a kingdom of luxury and comfort, not a kingdom, to use Paul's words, "of food and drink, but righteousness and peace and joy in the Holy Spirit" (Romans 14:17).

This is Christian joy. It is a journey not a destination. It is the happiness of those whose God is the Lord, the happiness of those who are free in Christ to be joyful.

Joyful, joyful, we adore thee,
God of glory, Lord of love;
hearts unfold like flowers before thee,
opening to the sun above.
Melt the clouds of sin and sadness,
drive the dark of doubt away;
Giver of immortal gladness,
fill us with the light of day.

Thou art giving and forgiving,
ever blessing, ever blest,
well-spring of the joy of living
ocean depth of happy rest!
Thou our Father, Christ our Brother,
all who live in love are thine;
teach us how to love each other,
lift us to the joy divine.[69]

Questions For Personal Reflection And/Or Group Discussion

1. How do you define "happiness"? What are its ingredients? Would you call yourself a happy person? If so, why? If not, why not?

2. If our happy moods are temporary, relative, and subjective, when are you the happiest? What makes you happy? What are the barriers to your happiness?

3. What is the relation between happiness and Christian joy?

4. Have you known people who are filled with Christian joy? What caused you to think that of them?

5. Do you agree that "Joy is the necessary sequence of our faith in God"?

6. How does Christ free us and enable us to be truly joyful?

Chapter Sixteen

Temper, Temper!
Free To Be Angry

Does the freedom for which we are set free in Jesus Christ include the freedom to be angry? Anyone who drives an automobile might question why it should be. People seem to be transformed into belligerent beasts when they get behind the wheel of a car. Road rage has become a major concern of public safety commissioners, police officers, psychologists, and all courteous drivers who have been the target of aggressive motorists and their abusive language and obscene gestures.

A decent, mild-mannered person could well wonder why anyone would suggest that the freedom to be angry is a desirable aspect of Christian freedom. It certainly would seem that it is not an unused freedom. Who of us has never felt the flush of anger? Whose conscience does not smart at the memory of unseemly displays of temper? Have we never fussed and fumed, churned and chafed, and felt the vials of wrath begin to boil?

We may have outgrown our childish tantrums, but we can still get our dander up readily enough. We still have our tiffs and tussles, and if we're not given to stormy outbursts and fits of temper, we surely have our moments of resentment and irritation, our sullen or irritable moods, when we are piqued, puckered, and provoked at the world in general or someone in particular.

Are not our bursts of anger an evidence more of weakness than of strength? In retrospect I am never happy with myself when I fly off the handle. So why should I suggest that Christian freedom includes the freedom to be angry? Why would the apostle Paul tell the Ephesians to be angry? Obviously there must be another kind of anger, a kind of anger that is desirable and appropriate, a kind of anger that in Jesus Christ we are free to express.

157

It is the kind of anger we see in our Lord himself, as he drove the money changers out of the temple, or castigated the Pharisees for their hypocrisy. "Woe to you, scribes and Pharisees, hypocrites! For you are like whitewashed tombs, which on the outside look beautiful, but inside they are full of the bones of the dead and of all kinds of filth.... You snakes, you brood of vipers! How can you escape being sentenced to hell?" (Matthew 23:27,33). These were the words of an angry man!

What is the difference between Jesus' anger and the kind of explosive anger we sometimes express or experience? The answer lies in the same paragraph in which Paul exhorted the Ephesians to be angry. "Put away from you all bitterness and wrath and anger and wrangling and slander, together with all malice..." (Ephesians 4:31). Such anger is a sin, the kind of anger Jesus warned against in his Sermon on the Mount: "You have heard that it was said to those of ancient times, 'You shall not murder'; and 'whoever murders shall be liable to judgment.' But I say to you that if you are angry with a brother or sister, you will be liable to judgment; and if you insult a brother or sister, you will be liable to the council; and if you say, 'You fool,' you will be liable to the hell of fire" (Matthew 5:21-22). Anger is the soil in which the seeds of hatred are sown. The angry person may be guilty of murder in her or his heart.

So Paul adds a caution to his injunction: "Be angry *but do not sin*..." (Ephesians 4:26a). In other words, do not let your anger breed bitterness and hatred. Do not let it lead to cruelty, or slander, or malice. Be angry, but be angry about the right things, not about some personal hurt, which is the anger of wounded pride. Such anger is like that of the President of the Women's Auxiliary, who refused to speak to any of the trustees of her church for five years, because they put up a towel rack in the kitchen without consulting her first.

Be angry, but not over some selfish desire, which is the anger of ambition and greed, or envy and covetousness, the jealous anger of the person who wants what someone else has. This kind of anger leads to hate and violence. Every so often we read about some irate husband who murders his estranged wife to prevent her from marrying another man.

158

Be angry, but not because you are impatient with something or someone, like the driver who curses every traffic signal and shouts obscenities at other motorists whose driving doesn't measure up to his or her standards.

Be angry, but not over personal failure or defeat, which is the anger of immaturity, like that of the poor sport who loses at bridge and takes it out on her partner, or the golfer who kicks his golf bag in a rage after missing a two-foot put.

Be angry, but about the right things. Admittedly, that is easier said than done, as the Greek philosopher Aristotle understood quite well. "Anybody can become angry," he said, "that is easy. But to be angry with the right person, and to the right degree, and at the right time, and for the right purpose, and in the right way, that is not within everybody's power and is *not* easy"[70]There are things every Christian should be angry about: child abuse and child pornography, battered women, international terrorism, drug trafficking, the denial of human rights to any group of people, the pollution of our environment, the rapacious waste of the earth's natural resources, the preoccupation of the media with sex and violence, ethnic cleansing, racial discrimination, religious persecution, political corruption, to name just a few. We have a right, indeed a Christian duty, to be angry about these things, about any form of injustice or cruelty, about crime and corruption, indecency and filth, dishonesty and deceit. This is the kind of anger Jesus felt, a righteous indignation about all forms of sin.

Not many people these days are really angry about sin. We are conditioned to be broad minded, so broad minded that our collective conscience has lost its cutting edge. In our desire to be open-minded we have gone too far, and we are paying the price for it. Someone has said there is nothing more open than a city dump; it will accept anything! We have had so much dirt slung at us from the magazine stands and the movie and television screens that we don't even duck any more. On the contrary, we pay billions of dollars every year to keep the filth merchants in business.

We hear more four-letter words in a school yard than we used to hear in a stock yard. Chastity is a belittled virtue among many young adults and sobriety a cause for scorn. It's hard to tell whether

America is on a drinking spree or a sex orgy, but when last seen Uncle Sam was heading down hill with a bottle in one arm and a sexy woman on the other.

What are Christians doing about all this? Not much, I fear, because we are too well assimilated into the secular culture. We're too involved in it to be angry about it. We may get angry, but not at the right things. We're angry about the crime rate because it affects *our* safety, but are we angry about the conditions which give rise to crime in the first place? We get angry at the legal system which sets offenders free, but are we angry about the inadequate programs and facilities there are for rehabilitating such persons? We get angry about teenage pregnancies and the loose sexual morality of not all but many young people, but are we angry about the disintegration of their moral values that is fueled by the movies and television programs they watch, the books and magazines they read, the music they listen to?

We must be angry about the right things, and we must be angry in the right way. There is a difference between expressing righteous indignation and losing one's temper, between a stern reprimand and a vindictive insult, between thoughtful consternation and uncontrolled rage. The trouble is we can't predict, let alone control, our angry outbursts. They happen too fast. A fit of temper is a knee-jerk reaction, an emotional response, not a rational decision. Something we don't like happens and we explode. We say or do things we're sorry for later. Sometimes the ways we express our anger are more sinful than the things we're angry about! The reaction is worse than the provocation, the retaliation more sinful than the offense.

> *When I am in my brittle mode,*
> *I'm more than likely to explode.*
> *When things are said behind my back,*
> *you'll find me quick to blow my stack.*
> *Just stick the knife in (and the fork!),*
> *if you want me to blow my cork.*
> *Or try to make me look the fool*
> *and watch how soon I lose my cool.*

To curb my temper I have tried
  till I have been fit to be tied.
I tell myself that I will stop,
  but then I go and blow my top
again, and that's the way it goes.
  When will it happen? Heaven knows![71]

The kind of anger that leads to hatred is not part of our freedom in Christ. There is a difference between hating the sin and hating the sinner. The former is right; the latter is wrong. We see this illustrated so clearly in Jesus' dealings with people, his rejection of sin on the one hand, and his compassionate forbearance for the sinner on the other.

Be angry but in the right way and with the right people. Too often we take out our anger on those we love, or those with whom we should be striving to get along. We forget who the enemy is.

Impatiently and hastily
in manner far from mild
too often I have scolded or
rebuked my little child,
and then discovered later on,
much to my deep chagrin,
that I was wrong and he was right.
My anger was the sin![72]

Paul suggests a further precautionary rule to avoid sinning in anger: "Do not let the sun go down on your anger" (Ephesians 4:26b). The literal meaning of the Greek word which Paul used here is "provocation" or "that which provokes anger." In other words, don't let the sun go down on the thing that caused your anser. What Paul was saying is that there is a limit to how long one should stay angry. Whatever caused that sudden outburst, that initial flare of temper, should not be allowed to fester. We should get it out of our system. This is also very sound and practical advice from a psychological standpoint, because all-consuming anger is an emotion that causes us to behave with an element of wildness or

161

lack of voluntary control. Our blood pressure goes up, our heart beat is more rapid, our responses are more explosive.

Such anger is, of course, a temporary condition, varying in degree and duration according to the nature of the stimulus. Rage can last only so long. It may recur again and again, but each fit of fury has a beginning and an end. If one continues to brood over whatever caused one's anger initially, the anger will turn into bitterness, hatred, and brooding resentment. Paul says we should not let this happen. We should not let the day pass without defusing the explosive. Then we are ready to deal with the problem in a reasonable and constructive manner. The provocation becomes the source of our determination to correct or reform or amend or reconcile.

Do not let the sun go down on your anger. Is there a better application of this rule than in the case of family squabbles? Husbands and wives quarrel, say things that hurt, things they do not really mean. How wrong it is to go to bed without making up. How sad when parents scold their children and send them off to bed in anger, like the father in this touching poem:

My little son, who look'd from thoughtful eyes,
and moved and spoke in quiet, grown-up wise,
having my law the seventh time disobey'd,
I struck him, and dismissed
with hard words and unkiss'd,
— his mother, who was patient, being dead.
Then, fearing lest his grief should hinder sleep,
I visited his bed,
but found him slumbering deep,
with darkened eyelids and their lashes yet
from his late sobbing wet.
And I, with moan
kissing away his tears, left others of my own;
for on a table drawn beside his head,
he had put, within his reach,
a box of counters and a red-veined stone,
a piece of glass abraded by the beach,

a bottle with bluebells,
and two French copper coins, ranged there with careful art,
to comfort his sad heart.[73]

Plutarch, the Greek moralist, said that the followers of Pythagoras had a rule that if ever they were provoked to anger or abusive language at one another, before the sun set, they would clasp hands and make up. Paul surely would have approved of this. So would the poet William Blake:

I was angry with my friend;
I told my wrath, my wrath did end.
I was angry with my foe;
I told it not, my wrath did grow.[74]

Some people, however, don't want to make up. They refuse to apologize or even to accept an apology. They don't want to be reconciled. They would rather indulge their anger. They enjoy licking their wounds, feeding the fires of resentment, like Robert Burns' "sulky, sullen dame . . . nursing her wrath to keep it warm."[75] Most of us, on the other hand, don't enjoy being angry; we just can't control it. We'd like to control it, but we can't.

Thus we have two main problems to solve in exercising our freedom to be angry: the problem of being angry about the right things and the problem of expressing our anger in the right way. How do we solve these problems? We can't solve them on our own, but with God's help we can! God can transform our conscience and sensitize us to be angry about the right things, and God can help us express our anger in the right way.

Not that we won't lose our temper now and then, as I mentioned earlier. I know I have a short fuse about some things. If you push the right button, you can get my dander up pretty quickly. But at least I am *aware* of that now, and that in itself is progress. And I think I'm more concerned than I used to be about the things I ought to be concerned about. I still have a long way to go, and so I keep on praying. That's the best way I know to seek God's help in learning to control our temper. Follow this three-word rule: Pray, pray, pray!

God in Christ has given us the freedom to be angry, and God through Jesus Christ can help us to channel our anger in the right direction and in appropriate ways. So Paul's advice is right on the mark: *"Be* angry, but do not sin, and do not let the sun go down on your anger."

> *Day by day, dear Lord,*
> *of thee three things I pray:*
> *to see thee more clearly,*
> *love thee more dearly,*
> *follow thee more nearly,*
> *day by day.*[76]

Questions For Personal Reflection
And/Or Group Discussion

1. Do you ever, sometimes, or often get angry? What kinds of things anger you? How long do you stay angry?

2. Does your anger ever get the best of you (i.e., cause you to lose your temper)? How do you vent your anger? Do you feel guilty afterwards?

3. Do you think our freedom in Christ should include the freedom to be angry? If not, why not? If so, about what kinds of things should a Christian be angry? When is anger a sin?

4. How should Christians express their anger? How should a Christian respond to the anger of others?

5. Have you ever known someone who harbored anger toward you? Is it hard for you to apologize, especially when you think you're right? What do you do when a person refuses to accept your apology?

6. If you have a disagreement with someone you love, who usually takes the initiative in seeking to be reconciled? Have you ever "let the sun go down on your anger"? What for you are the barriers to being reconciled to someone with whom you are angry?

Chapter Seventeen

The Shadow Of A Doubt
Free To Doubt

According to the Gallup studies of religion in America 95% of Americans year after year have said they believe in God. I would assume that anyone reading this book would want to be included in that figure.

At the same time I suspect that many if not most, even of those who would read a book like this, would admit that their faith has not always been without an element of doubt.

Surely if we have thought at all about some of the things we Christians are supposed to believe, we have felt the burden of unanswerable questions, perplexing paradoxes, conflicting interpretations, and unresolved ambiguities. If our minds have not been active, surely in our hearts we have at times sensed our spiritual inadequacy and wondered if the likes of us could ever be acceptable to God.

Or perhaps we have suffered pain and questioned the goodness of God, or trembled in the presence of death as if there were no life beyond the grave, or prayed as if our prayers were never heard. Perhaps we have professed our faith in Jesus Christ and wondered if our words were true, or participated in the Lord's Supper without knowing whether we really understood its meaning.

It is not an exaggeration, therefore, to say that even believers have doubts, whether or not we care to admit them —doubts about God, about Christ, about the Bible, about the Church, about ourselves. That will always be true as long as faith is what it is, for faith implies doubt. Faith and doubt are not opposites; they are corollaries. To accept something on faith implies, indeed *demands*, that the possibility exists it may or may not be so. If that possibility does not exist, if it is a matter of accepting what is proven, it ceases to be a matter of faith and becomes a matter of fact.

We cannot escape the necessity of having to accept most of what we believe on faith. This is true whether or not one believes in God. Does the thought never occur to an atheist, a *thinking* atheist, that he or she could be wrong? Those who deny God have their doubts as well as believers. That will always be the case in matters that cannot be proved, and to think otherwise is the height of ignorance and conceit. Atheists are less willing to admit their doubts than most people, but no less so than some militant believers are! If we are truly honest, we have to confess that there are times when our minds question what our hearts want to accept.

This is as it should be. If not, one's faith is riding for a fall. How tragic it can be for those who have never honestly faced their doubts, who are afraid to ask questions for fear there won't be answers, who won't open the door of their minds lest they find a skeptical skeleton in their spiritual closet! Such a timorous faith can be completely undone by an unexpected calamity. An unthinking faith is discomfited by the cold logic of science, flustered by the rational challenge of a thoughtful skeptic.

More to be pitied than those who have doubts but are afraid to face them, are those who refuse to admit they have any doubts at all. They have their faith wrapped up in a neat little package, with no loose ends. They have no patience with or sympathy for the person who dares to suggest that there are some questions which cannot be answered. Such a faith is the stuff of which bigots are made. The certainty of a bigot's belief is a false certainty, however, and to put more inclusively what the philosopher/statesman Francis Bacon, lord chancellor of England, wrote in one of his essays, "If we begin with certainties, we shall end in doubts...."[77]

Since the freedom to which we have been called in Jesus Christ includes the freedom to think, it follows that we also are free to doubt. As thinking Christians we should have the honesty to admit our doubts and the courage to face them, like the distraught father who cried to Jesus, "I believe; help my unbelief!" (Mark 9:24). Here was a man who wanted to believe, but doubted that he could. He had faith, but wondered if he had enough.

Yet the father was not the only one whose belief was uncertain in the revealing incident which Mark records in his Gospel. In fact, the characters in the story illustrate several different kinds of doubt, or perhaps we should say "degrees of unbelief." To reconstruct the scene briefly, Jesus and three of the disciples — Peter, James, and John — descended from the Mount of Transfiguration to find the other nine disciples surrounded by a great crowd. Some of the scribes were needling them about their inability to heal an apparently epileptic boy, whose father had come to them desperately seeking help. We can imagine the sarcastic remarks, the belittling sneers, the I-told-you-so jeers being hurled at the hapless disciples.

When they saw Jesus approaching, the crowd ran to greet him excitedly. Seeing the dispute, Jesus asked them what they had been arguing about. A man stepped forward and said, "Teacher, I brought you my son; for he has a spirit that makes him unable to speak; and whenever it seizes him, it dashes him down; and he foams and grinds his teeth and becomes rigid; and I asked your disciples to cast it out, but they could not do so" (Mark 9:17-18).

So that is what they were arguing about, and while they wrangled and fussed, making alibis for themselves and accusing one another, the poor lad was forgotten, his misery unrelieved, his suffering unheeded.

"You faithless generation ... how much longer must I put up with you?" was Jesus' exasperated response. The disciples were included in that remark, and the scribes, and the father, and the whole multitude about him. They were a spectrum of unbelief, a sliding scale of doubt. There was first of all the militant doubt of the scribes — antagonistic, defiant, willful disbelief. Theirs was the doubt of threatened, angry men, jealous, vengeful, cruel, the kind of doubt that crucified Jesus. Pontius Pilate recognized it in the chief priests, for as Matthew commented, "he realized that it was out of jealously that they had handed him over" (Matthew 27:18).

Now consider the epileptic child, who was the innocent subject of the controversy. We are told nothing of mute lad's faith, but we can assume he was either too young, or too ill, or both, to have known or thought about Jesus. For me he represents another kind of unbelief, call it the unbelief of insensibility. In his condition he was incapable of making a responsible decision.

There are too many like him in the world today, too many wretched souls who are too sick, too hungry, too poor even to think about God. They have all they can do to keep alive. Their abject poverty has robbed them of their dignity and stifled every spiritual instinct. How can one believe who is seized by the epilepsy of despair? Helpless victims of adversity, they are not against God, they simply cannot think about God at all. Nor will they be cured until someone brings them to the feet of the Master and he lays his healing hand upon them. The Church may open the doorway to hope for these forgotten people by ministering first to their bodily needs, just as Jesus first healed the disease-ridden boy. The kind of unbelief represented by these poor souls is an indictment not against them, but against those who allow such suffering to continue unattended.

Another level of unbelief is represented by the crowd of interested onlookers, the observers, standing on the borderline between belief and unbelief. They could be swayed either way, as they listened to the dispute between the disciples and the scribes, waiting to be convinced. They were like so much of the world today, riding the razor's edge of doubt, not quite believing, not quite denying, simply observing without committing themselves till they see which way the wind blows. Spiritually they are agnostics, morally they are conformists, politically they are opportunists. Forgetting all the evidences of God's power, the wonders of the past, they are inclined to hear only the strident voices of the scribes of the world, as they vacillate between faith and disbelief.

Still another degree of unbelief was that of the disciples. Here we move into the category of genuine faith, for theirs was not the militant disbelief of the scribes, nor the unknowing unbelief of the epileptic boy, nor the fence-rail unbelief of the onlookers. The disciples had honest doubts, doubt in themselves, doubt in their ability to do God's work. Like all of us, they had their ups and downs, their successes and their failures, their mountain-top moments of inspiration and their valleys of ineffectiveness. They had performed works of healing before. They had cast out demons, cured the deaf and the lame, cleansed lepers, but they could not help this epileptic boy.

Why not? They asked Jesus this question and he told them it could be done only by prayer. He did not mean by praying right then and there, for he himself did not pray over the boy. Rather he must have meant only as one lives a life of prayer, a life in tune with the mind of God, a life in constant communion with the source of divine power, can one hope to be an instrument of God's miraculous healing. The disciples had lost that power momentarily. Perhaps because of the antagonism of the crowd, or the necessity of having to perform a miracle under pressure, or because they were over-anxious, for whatever reason, they lacked the healing power of Christ. So it is with those who do not keep in tune with God, who alone can give one the power to act with the faith and confidence that comes through a life of prayer.

Then there is the father of the epileptic boy. He, too, had faith. He wanted to believe. He knew he must believe, but he realized in his heart of hearts that there was still an element of unbelief, the fear that this wonder worker might not be able to heal his son. That uncertainty was revealed when he said to Jesus, "If you are able to do anything, have pity on us and help us." Whereupon Jesus replied, "*If* you are able! All things can be done for the one who believes" (Mark 9:22-23). *If* you can. Do you doubt my power to help you? Do you not believe I am able?

Can we not see ourselves in this man? We offer up prayers for things we want, just in case. But we're not sure God can really help us. "If you can," said the father. "If *you* can," replied Jesus. I think that's how Jesus said it, meaning you must look within yourself first. "If *you* are able — All things can be done for the one who believes." How stunned the father must have been at those words. He undoubtedly thought he had done everything possible for his son. He had brought him to the disciples. He had brought him to the Master himself. Was there anything else he could do? Yes, said Jesus. You must have faith. You must believe I can heal your son.

Immediately the man cried, "I believe; help my unbelief!" I am sure the man was sincere when he said those words. Lord, I want to believe, but I don't know if I can believe. I know there is

171

unbelief within me. Help me, Lord. Help me in spite of my unbelief. Help me overcome my unbelief. That should be our prayer, should it not? For Jesus demands the same of us. If we want his help with our problems, we must have faith that he can help us, but it's that very fact that makes us doubt the quality of our faith. Once again we see the paradox of faith, the tension between the faith we know we must have and the doubt we know we do have, between our responsibility to have faith and our dependence upon God for the gift of faith, between belief and unbelief, between certainty and uncertainty, between what we want to be and what we are. This is the source of our doubt, and so we cry, "Lord, I believe; help my unbelief!"

But remember this: Jesus did heal the epileptic boy! The father's honest doubt was good enough for Jesus. Therein lies our hope, and therein lies our freedom to doubt. The important thing is not that we have no doubts, but that we are free to admit our doubts; not whether we believe completely, but whether we want to believe in spite of our unbelief. For the Christ we are struggling to believe in will not turn us away because of our honest doubts.

If we need any reassurance of that, we have only to recall the story of Thomas, the disciple whose name has been forever linked with doubt. Yet it was that same doubting Thomas who was the first of all the disciples to confess the full divinity of Jesus. He had doubted because he was not present the first time Jesus appeared to the disciples in the upper room after the resurrection. But he was there the second time, and when Jesus held out his hands to him and told him to put his hand on the place where the sword had pierced him, Thomas, with all the conviction, joy, and relief of a yearning soul that has found the truth, exclaimed, "My Lord and my God!"

So, did Jesus reject Thomas because he had doubted? By no means, because his was not the doubt of the Pharisees — cynical, obstinate, bitter; nor the doubt of Rome — indifferent, bored, superior. Nor was it the doubt of those who demanded a sign only that they might scoff at it. No, his was a seeking doubt, critical but sincere, uncertain but willing to be convinced. Thomas had the earnest doubt of a person longing to believe, and when such a mind is convinced, the result is an unshakeable faith.

Jesus' response to Thomas underscores the marvelous truth that Jesus never objected to questions, when the person who asked them was sincere. What a relief to know that the freedom to which we have been called in Jesus Christ includes even the freedom to doubt! There should be room in every church for people like Thomas, people with doubts, people who ask honest questions, thinking people with critical minds but loving hearts.

Faith without doubt is not faith at all. But it must be a seeking doubt, not a stubborn, arrogant, militant disbelief. Jesus loved Thomas, even though he was a doubter, because when Thomas did see, he believed. God in Christ always responds to those who are earnestly seeking to know the truth about him. "When you search for me, you will find me; if you seek me with all your heart, I will let you find me, says the LORD" (Jeremiah 29:13-14a).

We are not given the proof that was offered to Thomas. We cannot see the print of the nails in Jesus' hands nor feel the wound in his side. But we can know him, nevertheless. We can confess him as our Lord and our God, and when we do, we are blessed all the more. "Have you believed because you have seen me?" Jesus asked Thomas. "Blessed are those who have not seen and yet have come to believe" (John 20:29).

In the light of this discussion of our freedom to doubt, these two stanzas from a gospel hymn heard by millions at Billy Graham Crusades should take on new meaning:

> *Just as I am, though tossed about*
> *with many a conflict, many a doubt,*
> *fightings and fears within, without,*
> *O Lamb of God, I come, I come!*

> *Just as I am! Thou wilt receive,*
> *wilt welcome, pardon, cleanse, relieve;*
> *Because thy promise I believe,*
> *O Lamb of God, I come, I come!*[78]

Questions For Personal Reflection And/Or Group Discussion

1. Have you ever had doubts about God, or Christ, or the Bible, or unanswered questions about the Christian faith in general? If so, what kinds of doubts or questions?

2. In the Apostles' Creed Christians profess the following: *I believe in God the Father Almighty, Maker of heaven and earth; and in Jesus Christ his only Son our Lord; who was conceived by the Holy Ghost, born of the Virgin Mary, suffered under Pontius Pilate, was crucified, dead, and buried; he descended into hell; the third day he rose again from the dead; he ascended into heaven, and sitteth on the right hand of God the Father Almighty; from thence he shall come to judge the quick and the dead. I believe in the Holy Ghost; the holy catholic Church; the communion of saints; the forgiveness of sins; the resurrection of the body; and the life everlasting. Amen*

   Do you understand and believe everything in that creed?

3. How do you understand the relation between doubt and faith?

4. When is your faith strongest? When is it weakest?

5. Is the idea that in Christ we are free to doubt disturbing to you or encouraging? Why? Is it helpful or unhelpful to other people to know that believers have doubts? Elaborate.

6. What should and can you do about your doubts?

Chapter Eighteen

Confirming Evidence
Free To Be Sure

When it comes to buying things, most of us follow the old maxim that "seeing is believing." And when it comes to ideas that stretch our credulity, we're all from Missouri: we have to be shown to be convinced.

But in the realm of religion, this presents a problem. For how can we really be sure there is a God, if as John says, "no one has ever seen God" (I John 4:12)? You can't prove the existence of God algebraically. There is no scientific experiment that can convince an unbeliever of God's existence.[79]

Does that mean, then, that there is no valid basis for faith, no assurance that what we have believed to be true is really true? Are those who preach and teach about God perpetrating an illusion? Are preachers' sermons only a form of mental prestidigitation, and we poor believers the inveigled victims of a clever "slight of mind'? Is faith only a fabrication of our will to believe and all religious faith mere wishful thinking, as the skeptics charge? Are we being bluffed, blinded, and bamboozled by a beautiful bubble that will burst on the prickly branches of modern science?

There have always been and there probably always will be those who shout an angry Yes! to such questions, those who like Karl Marx look upon religion as "the opium of the people."[80] "Religion is comparable to a childhood neurosis," asserted Sigmund Freud.[81] And among the many barbs hurled at religion by the cynical journalist H. L. Mencken was the blunt accusation that religion is simply "a concerted effort to deny the most obvious realities."[82] Because we believers cannot prove our point to them by logical argument, we resign ourselves to the inescapable conclusion that in the sunlight of faith we can never be beyond the shadow of doubt.

But if we are to have any kind of spiritual security, any confidence that the future has meaning, then we have to be sure there *is* a God. Faith in God must be based on more than guesswork, more than mere supposition. Our sense of security has to be based on some assurance that what we believe to be true is indeed true. Is it possible to know there is a God, a personal God, a God who is responsive to us and to whom we are responsible? Given our freedom to doubt, can we really be sure?

This is an immensely important question for anyone who is worried about an unbelieving friend or relative, or who is wondering about how to be a faithful witness or a more effective communicator of one's faith. It is a tremendously important question, too, for those of us who call ourselves believers yet have to struggle with our doubts. What if we Christians are wrong? Have you taken that question seriously? What if Jesus was only a man, and the resurrection only a myth? What if there is no God, no Christ, no Holy Spirit? Can we really be sure?

Yes, we can be sure! With all the conviction I possess I say we can be sure. Not that our understanding of God will ever be complete, because it will not be. Not that we won't have questions about God, because we will. Not that we can prove God to someone who doesn't want to believe, because we can't. Not that we ever escape entirely the presence of doubt, because it is always lurking in the wings, and that is as it should be in the realm of faith.[83] But we can be sure of God, nevertheless. We can know the reality of God. The freedom to which we are called in Jesus Christ includes the freedom to be sure.

There is a dimension of knowledge that is not based on sensory perception, that is not subject to scientific experimentation, that is not dependent upon rational analysis. This kind of knowledge defies dissection. It cannot be demonstrated or verified mathematically. A mother knows she loves her child, though she can't distill her affection in a test tube.

So it is with the knowledge of God. Like Job, I can know my Redeemer lives, though I can't prove it. Sometimes I wonder what God must think of those people who sit around debating God's existence, as if God's existence depended upon their ability to prove

176

it! They're like ants in an elephant cage, debating whether or not there are such things as elephants!

The reason some of us are not as sure as we ought to be, indeed as we are free to be, is that we start from the wrong premise. The very idea of trying to prove God exists implies that God may not exist. We ought to start where the ancient biblical writers started, with the premise that God is. The writer of the Book of Genesis didn't try to prove the existence of God. He simply declared, "In the beginning God created the heaven and the earth..." (Genesis 1:1).

That is where we should begin — with the assumption of God. Then we'll see how much evidence there is to support that premise, for there is much more reason to believe in God than there is to deny God. Thomas Aquinas' ingenious arguments for the existence of God will not convince a militant skeptic, but they do support the convictions of anyone who already believes in God.

I have in my files an article written by a once-popular radio/television evangelist which is entitled "Seven Proofs for the Existence of God." Such arguments are advanced by people who already believe, and they speak to people who already believe. But they could never be the basis of my assurance. For one thing, such arguments, like the so-called Thomistic proofs, all presuppose what they are trying to prove. If my belief in God depended on anybody's arguments, including my own, I could no longer believe in God! I cannot prove the existence of God to myself or to anyone else!

Nor is my assurance based on the testimony of the many scientists who see evidences of a Divine Hand in the order and purpose of the universe. All nature seems to point to a divine Creator, but my certainty in not here either, nor in the conviction that there has to be a First Cause (namely God) or an answer to the ultimate Why (namely God).

The countless millions of believers down through the ages, men and women who were sure about God, sure enough to die for their faith, are impressive, but they are not the basis of my assurance. Take Job, for example. In the midst of his affliction, in the pit of despair, having lost his possessions, his family, his health, this suffering, sore-ridden, beaten man could say "I know my Redeemer lives!" He didn't say, "I guess my Redeemer lives," or "I hope my

177

Redeemer lives." He said "I *know* that my Redeemer lives!" (Job 19:25).

One cannot but be impressed by such an affirmation of faith. Yet this is still not an adequate basis for *me* to be sure, for in the sphere of faith another's knowledge is insufficient authority for me. I am impressed by it but not persuaded, encouraged but not convinced. A woman said to me recently in a seminar, "Well, I believe, because my mother taught me to believe, when I was a child!"

"Wonderful!" I replied. "But why do you believe *now*? Do you still believe in Santa Claus?"

Not to be undone by that response, a man in the group declared, almost belligerently, "Well, I believe in Jesus because of the Bible, which is sharper than a two-edged sword. If the Bible says it, I believe it!"

Well, I believe the Bible, too! As a believer, I know it is an inspired book, a difficult book but an inspired book. The Bible is difficult because, as I emphasized in Chapter 11, it doesn't always mean what it says. It means what it *means*. Anyone who can read can tell you what it says; the challenge is to know what it means, for there are parts that are very difficult to understand, parts about which the best biblical scholars can differ in their interpretation. Even Simon Peter had trouble interpreting Paul's letters. "There are some things in them hard to understand," wrote Peter (II Peter 3:16). If he had trouble understanding Paul's letters, how much more can we.

But there are plenty of passages that make it abundantly clear who Jesus is, and what he can do for us, and what he has done for us. "I write these things," said John, "to you who believe in the name of the Son of God, so that you may *know* that you have eternal life" (I John 5:13). The Bible was written that *we who believe* might know. It is an amazing compilation of stories, prophecies, prayers, proverbs, parables, philosophy, history, songs, letters, wise sayings, instructions, through which God's purpose for humankind is unfolded. The Bible is for us a written record of God's mighty acts, culminating in the coming of Jesus Christ. I would never disparage the Bible, through which God speaks to me every time I read it.

Still I must say that I don't believe in God because of the Bible; I believe the Bible, because I already believed in God! I would never want to belittle the Bible to anyone, but I want to encourage thinking people, people who wish to be sure about their faith, to realize that not even the Bible will convince someone who doesn't want to believe. If that were all it took to convince someone, then any atheist could be converted simply by requiring him or her to read the Bible. But anyone who has tried to use the Bible as a hammer to pound someone into believing knows that it doesn't work that way. Only those who already believe in God know that the Bible is the word of God. Nonbelievers don't accept the authority of the Bible.

When I say this, some indignant person inevitably retorts, "Well, the Bible is the Word of God, whether they believe it or not!" What that well-meaning Christian doesn't understand is that such a retort is a faith statement. That the Bible is the word of God is not self-evidently true to the person who doesn't believe in God.

The Bible alone is not enough to bring that "blessed assurance" we sing about.[84] What, then, is the ultimate basis of our assurance? What is the secret of our certainty? There is only one way to be sure, and that is through one's own personal experience of God. It was fine for *Paul* to say "I know the one in whom I have put my trust," but do *I* know in whom I put *my* trust? Job's knowledge of God won't help me until I, too, can know that *my* Redeemer lives. John can write in order that we may know, but his words will have no authority for me unless the Holy Spirit *convinces* me, convinces *me*, of their truth.

Mark my words: I am not saying that my experience is proof of the existence of God. I am saying that my experience of God is *the basis of my conviction*, of my assurance. I believe in God because I know God personally. The God I believe in has given me the faith to believe. My experience is not the basis for other people's assurance, any more than theirs is for me. I can't prove God's existence, but I know God exists, because God is real to me.

So I start from there. I know it is an assumption of faith. But on the basis of that assumption I can now understand that the Bible is indeed the word of God and the authoritative rule for faith and practice. The Bible, the testimonies of other believers, the witness of the Church, the various arguments for the existence of God are all part of the confirming evidence of my faith assumption, confirming evidence of the truth of that assumption.

Now I understand who Jesus is, because I've come to know him as my personal Lord and Savior. The Holy Spirit speaking through the Scriptures has convinced me that Jesus is who he said he was, and who the New Testament and the Church have affirmed him to be. I believe in him because he is real to me.

I know that faith in God is a gift. It is not something I can make myself have; it is something I find myself with. There's a world of difference between knowing *about* God and knowing God personally, between talking about God and talking with God. Most of those who read this book understand that completely. But some readers may be thinking, How do I go about knowing God? The only way to know God is to obey God. The only way to know Christ is to follow him. "By this we may be sure that we know him, if we obey his commandments," wrote John. "By this we may be sure that we are in him: whoever says, 'I abide in him,' ought to walk as he walked" (I John 2:3,5).

In other words, if you really want to know God, then start acting as if there is a God and live the kind of life God would want you to live. If you obey God, you will come to know God. Do you really want to know Christ? Then follow him; serve him, and you will come to believe in him.

So the prior question is, Do you really *want* to know him? Do you really *want* to be sure? If you do, then hear this good news: If you want to, you can! In fact, if you really want to, you already know God! The God you are struggling to believe in has given you the faith to *want* to believe! If you want to know God, if you want to know Jesus Christ, you are a seeker, and God never turns away those who seek him. "If you seek me with all your heart, I will let you find me, says the LORD" (Jeremiah 29:13-14). "Ask, and it will be given you," said Jesus; "seek, and you will find; knock, and it will be opened to you" (Matthew 7:7). If you are a seeker, the chances are that you have already met God. Perhaps you just haven't recognized God.

If you aren't sure about it, the first thing to do is to think about what could be evidences of God in your own life. Whence came the inspiration for some act of kindness, some deed of mercy, some expression of love — kindness, mercy, and love of which you didn't even know you were capable? Whence came your capacity to forgive someone you never thought you could forgive? Whence came your awareness of your need to be forgiven, the noble impulse to say "I'm sorry"? Who gave you the strength to carry that heavy burden of grief or pain? Those spontaneous urges to pray, what prompted them? Those sudden glimpses of truth, those clarifying insights that exceed your own wisdom, where did they come from? Those serendipitous occurrences that the world calls coincidences, why did they happen the way they did, and when they did? Are they not too amazing to have happened by chance? Are they mere coincidence or are they providential? The person you know whose life seems completely changed by the radiance of a new commitment, whence came that transforming power?

What does it take to make some people believe in God? How many miracles of God's transforming power? How many tokens of God's love and mercy? How many examples of God's wisdom and grace? God has indeed touched their lives, but some folks just haven't given God the credit. The difference between believers and nonbelievers is a matter of who gets the credit. Faith gives the credit to God. Some people just haven't recognized the God who has already been working in their lives. God was the Stranger they passed without looking. They did not know their Redeemer's name.

I believe in God because of the reality of God's presence in my life. I know what God has done for me personally. I know that God called me into ministry, and that God has continued to work in my life in natural and often miraculous ways over the years. A day never passes without some new evidence of God's grace, love, and providential care. I'm sure there is a God, because God is so real to me. I would not be writing this book, if I did not know my Redeemer lives.

Job's words have special meaning for Christians, because, as John says, "we know that the Son of God has come and has given us understanding so that we may know him who is true" (I John

5:20a). In Jesus Christ we are free to be sure. We need no longer guess or speculate about God, because Jesus has shown us what God is like. He has "brought life and immortality to light through the gospel" (II Timothy 1:10).

"I and the Father are one," Jesus said (John 10:30). "Whoever has seen me has seen the Father" (John 14:9). No one has ever seen God, that is true. "It is God the only Son, who is close to the Father's heart, who has made him known" (John 1:18).

Yes, Christ has come, and because he lives, you and I are free to have a personal relationship with a living Lord. As John says, "We are in him who is true, in his Son Jesus Christ. He is the true God and eternal life" (I John 5:20b).

So if you really want to know God, then get to know Jesus Christ, who is the way, and the truth, and the life — the way to God, the truth about God, and the life with God. If seeing is believing, if believing is seeing, then look at Jesus. In him you are free to be sure!

If you want to know what God is like,
*   then look at Jesus, friend.*
He came as God in human form
*   that you might apprehend.*
If you want to know what God expects
*   of you, then listen well*
to the words of Jesus, who alone
*   can all your fears dispel.*
If you want to know what God can do,
*   then look at Jesus, friend.*
If you want to know what God has done
*   for you, you'll comprehend,*
when you've looked at Jesus' life and work,
*   and see the way he died,*
and can understand it was for you
*   that he was crucified.*[85]

Questions For Personal Reflection And/Or Group Discussion

1. Given our freedom to doubt and admitting that there is much about our faith that we don't understand and can't explain, do you think it is possible to be absolutely sure there is a God and that Jesus is the Son of God and the Savior of the world? Why do you or don't you?

2. If a person said to you, "If you can prove to me that Jesus is the Christ, then I'll believe in him," how would you respond?

3. Admitting that our affirmations of faith are not self-evident to a non-believer, what evidence can you think of to support your belief in a personal God?

4. What part has the Bible played in your faith development?

5. How would you describe your relationship with Jesus Christ? If you have accepted Christ as your personal Lord and Savior, how did you arrive at that conviction? What do you know for sure about Jesus?

6. If you are convinced that what you believe about God and Christ is true, how do you feel about and relate to people of other faiths who may be equally convinced thtat what they believe is The Truth?

Chapter Nineteen

Come What May
Free To Be Secure

September 11, 2001: a date that no American will ever forget.. New York City glistens in the early morning sunlight, with a clear blue sky providing a perfect backdrop for the familiar skyline. Suddenly the unthinkable happens. We are called to our television screens to stare in horrified disbelief, as terrorist hijackers crash first one then another fully fueled, cross-country commercial jet into the twin towers of the World Trade Center. A third plane slams into the Pentagon, blasting a huge hole in that symbol of America's military power. A fourth hijacked plane plunges to the ground in Western Pennsylvania, its deadly mission foiled by the heroic intervention of the passengers.

We weep as we watch people leaping to their death from 90 or 100 stories above the New York streets, rather than perish in the flames. Then our sobs become a gasp, as the twin towers, symbols of America's commercial power, come crashing to the ground, wreaking havoc and destruction on adjacent buildings and everything beneath. Thousands flee the billowing smoke and falling debris. Many are able to make their way down the pitch black stairwells to safety, as fire fighters rush up the stairs to their death. The heroes become the victims, that the victims might be saved. Thousands are blown to bits by the explosions or crushed beneath tons of steel and concrete.

In an instant thus were we Americans made frightfully aware of our vulnerability, and now we wonder who can ever feel secure in a world like this? In the best of times, natural disasters, accidents, unforeseen calamities can swiftly and unexpectedly shatter our ordered lives. Add to this the violence and destruction that human beings and nations inflict upon each other. Wars continue to

185

take their gruesome toll. As Americans reeled from the devastating impact of the most deadly terrorist attack in our nation's history, many were feeling for the first time how our allies and enemies must have felt in World War II. Before September 11, 2001, it would have been difficult if not impossible for younger Americans to imagine the degree of destruction the Allied bombing raids inflicted on Germany.

On the night of August 3, 1943, the people of Hamburg, Germany, sat in their bomb shelters waiting for the RAF raid they knew would come. Outside the air was still. Grim and silent the darkened city lay, hardened by more than a hundred previous attacks. Hamburg, with the best civil defense organization in the world, was prepared for its nightly beating.

But not for such a night as this. The British fliers in one mass incendiary attack transformed the city into a roaring inferno, described in lurid detail by Martin Caidin in one of his earlier books.[86] Twelve hundred separate fires converging toward a common center created a firestorm that sent flames shooting fifteen thousand feet in the air. The temperature at the periphery of the storm reached 1472 degrees Fahrenheit, as the superheated air soared to 40,000 feet above the earth, causing winds of double hurricane force. Six square miles of Hamburg were completely devastated. Nothing in that area, not even an insect, survived. 80,000 persons lost their lives, and 130,000 more were injured, during that night of flaming horror. Following the raid the city had to be abandoned, for there were no services, no utilities, no light, no gas, no water, nothing. It is hard to imagine, but the fire bombing of Dresden was even more destructive!

Two years later the first atom bombs exploded over the cities of Hiroshima and Nagasaki, Japan, leaving two hundred thousand people dead or injured. Incredibly, more people were killed in fire bombings of Tokyo than in either of those two cities. I was in Tokyo right after V-J Day and saw the devastation of that city with my own eyes. The bombing of Hiroshima and Nagasaki ended our war with Japan, but the armament race went on, as the threat of international Communism became the dominant political issue in the so-called Free World, with both sides stock piling their nuclear

arsenals. Along came the hydrogen bomb, and soon we were testing bombs that made the A-bomb look like a firecracker. Premier
Nikita Kruschchev boasted of the Soviet Unions's ability to produce bombs of 100 megatons; that's one hundred million tons of
TNT! The destructive power of such a bomb is incomprehensible.
It would cause second degree burns up to a radius of 75 miles from
the detonation point, third degree burns up to 60 miles. It would
blast a crater in the earth's crust 500 feet deep and more than a mile
in diameter. For several miles in all directions there would be nothing left. Destruction from the heat and shock wave would be ter-
rific for much greater distances, and beyond this there would be
the on-going danger from the radio-active fall-out.

All the fire departments in the world would not be able to put
out the fires started by one hydrogen bomb. And if and when a
nuclear attack ever occurs, there will not be just one bomb! The
first attack would have to destroy the enemy completely to avoid
retaliation. And now there are many nuclear powers, and who knows
when some terrorist group might decide to use The Bomb, or resort to germ warfare, or some other means of mass destruction.

I remember in the early 1960s, during the Cold War, hearing
the radio broadcasts of Martin Caidin, in which he made the case
for a realistic civil defense program. He warned that we were woe-
fully unprepared for a nuclear attack. I telephoned Mr. Caidin right
after one of his broadcasts from radio station WNEW, New York,
and talked at length with him about the implications of the then
accelerating nuclear arms build up. After listening to his alarming
statistics, I asked him, "Where, then, is our hope of security in this
world?"

"There is no real security," he replied. "We human beings have
always searched for security, but we have never found it."

Now, many years later, I can agree with at least part of Martin
Caidin's philosophical observation: individuals and nations have
always searched for security. In those early Cold War years people
were building bomb shelters in their backyards, their self-styled
security against a nuclear attack. It would seem that deep down
within them what many people desire above all else in these violent times is security. In countries like South Africa, where crime

and corruption are rampant at present, people long for security. Those living in our American urban jungles yearn to escape to the safety of the suburbs, only to discover that suburbia has its problems, too.

Since the break-up of the Soviet Union, we Americans are less paranoid about the threat of Communism than we once were, but national security is a constant issue, and politicians still argue about the defense budget.

As individuals we seek security from the moment we're born. An infant feels safe in its mother's arms. A young lad makes a hero of his Dad. When we're older we seek security in family ties and friendships, in savings accounts and pension plans, in health and accident insurance and regular physical check-ups, in retirement communities with permanent health care provided. Congress even enacted legislation to help meet this basic human need, and they called it "social security."

But is our ultimate security to be found in these things? When I was a child I felt safe if either of my parents was near. But my parents are dead now. The friendships that meant so much to me as a boy have faded into the mist of memory. I have lost too many friends to seek security in any person, and I have seen too much of life to try to ground my security in the things of this world. Even the social security system is in financial jeopardy. Soon they may be calling it "social insecurity."

Jesus said, "Do not store up for yourselves treasures on earth, where moth and rust consume and where thieves break in and steal..." (Matthew 6:19). The Dow Jones may hit record highs, but there can always be another Black Monday[87], and there could always come another Great Depression.[88] The gross national product can soar to new heights, but there are still far too many people unemployed. The United States may have the highest per capita income in the world, but there are still millions of Americans living below the poverty line. We may have a noble constitution, but there are still some dishonest politicians. We may be a free country, but our kids aren't free of drug pushers, and many of our schools are not free of violence. We may have the biggest stockpile of guided missiles and build what we think is an impervious missile defense shield, but they are no guarantee against terrorism.

There is no security in the things of this world, though humankind has ever sought to find it there. France felt secure behind the Maginot Line, but it did not stop the armies of Hitler. The walls of Jericho came tumbling down. The invincible Spanish Armada was not invincible. It sought to destroy the British fleet but was itself destroyed. Someone has said the Spaniards failed to win by only two ships: seamanship end marksmanship!

There is no safe airplane. There is no unwreckable train. There is no accident-proof automobile. There is no unsinkable ship.

> *O they built the ship Titanic, and when it was through,*
> *they said "This is the ship that the water will never go*
> *through."*
> *But the Lord he raised his hand,*
> *said "This ship, it shall not stand."*
> *It was sad when that great ship went down.*[89]

Our security is not in our unlimited natural resources, for our resources are not unlimited. Our security is not in our national wealth, for that too is limited by factors beyond anyone's control, including the Federal Reserve Board. Our security is not in our nuclear stockpile, nor our missile bases, nor our nuclear powered submarines. We need to learn from the Psalmist, who wrote "A king is not saved by his great army; a warrior is not delivered by his great strength. The war horse is a vain hope for victory, and by its great might it cannot save" (Psalm 33:16-17).

There is no ultimate security in the things which human beings and nations are predisposed to turn to for security. Our security is not in the benevolence of any government, nor in the soundness of any economy, nor in the persuasive power of any philosophical idea. So was Martin Caidin right after all? Is there no security?

Indeed there is! "The LORD is my rock, and my fortress, and my deliverer..." (Psalm 18:2a). Our security is in God, not in our national wealth, not in our military power, not in our treaties, or in NATO, or the United Nations, not in any self-righteous belief that

America is God's kingdom on earth and that capitalism is destined by God to triumph ultimately over socialism, not in anything else but Almighty God. "Blessed is the nation whose God is the LORD" (Psalm 33:12).

By no means am I implying that all these things are bad in themselves, that we should not belong to NATO or the United Nations, or that socialism is better than capitalism. What I am saying is that there is no ultimate security in these things. Our security is in God.

But what is the nature of this security? It is by no means an escape hatch from the tribulations of the world. It is not a celestial passport to peace and prosperity. It is not a guarantee of immediate triumph, for God is the LORD of *all* nations. "The LORD looks down from heaven; he sees all humankind ... and observes all their deeds" (Psalm 33:13,15b). As Americans we have no right to assume that God is on our side. Our only concern should be that we are on God's side. Our security is not in the vain assurance that God will spare America, but in the confident trust that "in everything God works for good for those who love God, who are called according to his purpose" (Romans 8:28).

Psalm 18 is an out-pouring of praise to God for David's deliverance from his enemies. It is the thankful song of a victorious king, who gives God the credit for his triumph. But the security which we seek from God is not triumph in battle, though we may pray for it. It is not the expectation that our side will win, though we hope it does. It is rather triumph over futility, triumph over fear, triumph over the hopelessness that any search for self-made security must inevitably lead to, triumph over the dark despair that resigns the affairs of the world to the fortuitous whims of chance.

Those who are called to freedom in Jesus Christ can have this kind of security. *Those who are free to be sure are free to be secure.* God has given us that freedom, the right to feel secure — not from death, or sickness, or poverty, or hardship, or sorrow, or pain, or suffering, or temptation, but secure in the knowledge that God is Lord of all humankind and of all nations. Come what may, God's will shall be done, his kingdom will come on earth, as in heaven. This is our security. One who has that assurance need no longer seek security in the ephemeral things of this world. In Jesus Christ we are free to put our trust, our hope, our confidence in God.

But some Christians have not availed themselves of that freedom. They act as if there is no security, or they delude themselves into thinking they can find it somewhere else. Then tragedy strikes and they are undone. They think God has let them down, when what has let them down is their own false security. "The LORD is ... my rock in whom I take refuge, my shield and the horn of my salvation, my stronghold" (Psalm 18:2b-c). If God is our stronghold, we are secure.

"But how do I get this security?" you might ask. It's not a matter of *getting* it. It is a matter of *having* it! "... This is the victory that overcomes the world, our faith," said John. "Who is it that overcomes the world but the one who believes that Jesus is the Son of God?" (I John 5:4-5). If you believe in Jesus Christ, then you are free to be secure, for your security rests in the conviction that in Christ God has demonstrated the love God has toward us. "For God so loved the world that he gave his only Son, that everyone who believes in him may not perish but may have eternal life" (John 3:16).

This is our security, the security of faith, the security that enables us to say with Paul that "neither death, nor life, nor angels, nor principalities, nor things present, nor things to come, nor powers, nor height, nor depth, nor anything else in all creation will be able to separate us from the love of God in Christ Jesus our Lord" (Romans 8:38-39).

This is the security those who are in Christ are free to have, the only real security in this insecure world of ours. For sooner or later misfortune can come to every one of us: a business reversal, the loss of a job, a serious accident, the death of a loved one, a natural disaster, a terminal illness we never wanted, a war we never started, a fire we always dreaded. Trouble can come unannounced and unexpected, at home, at work, at play. Sooner or later we realize how precarious is the precious gift of life and how insecure we really are, apart from God. "The cords of death encompassed me; the torrents of perdition assailed me," wailed the Psalmist (Psalm 1:84).

As I think about the congregations I have served, the faces of so many people I knew and loved are in my mind's eye, people whose heartaches and sorrows I was privileged to share and now recall so vividly. I see a man who had to leave his native land, having lost his home, his business, all of his possessions. Wherein lay his security under an oppressive government whose reign of terror betrayed its false promises? The Lord had been his stronghold, and thanks to the support of a loving congregation, he and his family made a new start in America.

I see the faces of husbands who lost their wives, and of wives who lost their husbands. They, too, have been sustained by faith. As I write this a dear friend is dying of acute leukemia. He and his wife are facing his impending death with complete confidence in the goodness of the God they have loved so long and served so well.

I see the face of a loving wife being told by a surgeon that her husband had died unexpectedly on the operating table. Whence came her serenity but from God? I see a young couple giving thanks through their tears for the strength they had found in their church, strength enough to bear the shock of discovering their infant son dead in his crib. I can see an 80-year old blind man sitting in his wheel chair in his tiny one-room apartment, his diseased body throbbing with constant pain, praising God and thanking God for his health!

Some families have more than their share of tragedy and sorrow. Certainly the Kennedys are one of those families, and the entire world grieved with them on each tragic occasion. But as a pastor I discovered across the years that behind *every* front door there are problems and needs, and every family has experienced sorrow and suffering, in different ways and to varying degrees. To those who feel they have been spared such pain, I can only say "Praise God for that!" but sooner or later everyone's safe little world is bound to be rocked by the stormy winds of life.

When that happens, some walk erect, some buckle under the strain. Some carry on, others give up. What makes the difference? The difference is God. Those who bear adversity with a peace of mind that unbelievers simply cannot understand are those who put their hope and trust in God. "In my distress I called upon the LORD," said the Psalmist; "to my God I cried for help. From his temple he heard my voice, and my cry to him reached his ears" (Psalm 18:6). They have hope for the future, because they know that the future is in God's hands. They can face death with confidence, because they know that, come what may, nothing can separate us from the love of God, which is in Christ Jesus our Lord.

The freedom to which we are called in Jesus Christ includes freedom from fear, the freedom to enjoy a sense of security that the unbelieving world can never attain, the freedom that comes only through faith in Almighty God. "The LORD is my light and my salvation; whom shall I fear? The LORD is the stronghold of my life; of whom shall I be afraid?" (Psalms 27:1). Come what may, in Jesus Christ we are secure! And so we sing:

> *I know not what the future hath of marvel or surprise,*
> *assured alone that life and death his mercy*
> *underlies.*
> *And if my heart and flesh are weak to bear an untried pain,*
> *the bruised reed he will not break, but strengthen and*
> *sustain.*
> *And so beside the Silent Sea I wait the muffled oar;*
> *No harm from him can come to me on ocean or on*
> *shore.*
> *I know not where his islands lift their fronded palms in*
> *air;*
> *I only know I cannot drift beyond his love and care.*[90]

* * * * *

The peace of God, which passes all human understanding, keep your heart and mind in the knowledge and love of God and of his Son Jesus Christ, and the blessing of God Almighty, Father, Son, and Holy Spirit, be with you and all whom you love, and with the world which God created and still loves, now and forever. Amen.

Questions For Personal Reflection
And/Or Group Discussion

1. Have you ever felt insecure? What were the circumstances that caused your feeling of insecurity? Does that feeling persist, or have you overcome it?

2. Insecurity is related to fear. What are your greatest fears? How do you deal with them?

3. When do you feel most secure? What part does your faith play in your feeling of security or insecurity?

4. How does our faith in Jesus Christ free us to be secure? How would you describe our security in Christ to someone who asks you what you mean by it?

5. The statement was made that "those who are free to be sure are free to be secure." How do you understand the relation between our freedom to be sure and our freedom to be secure?

6. Parents who understand the meaning of Christian security and who themselves have a sense of security, need to pass it on to their children and grandchildren. How would you go about doing that?

Where Do We Go From Here?
Some Final Questions

1. What insights have you gained about yourself as a result of these readings and your reflections and/or discussions? What have you learned about others?

2. Have you discovered things about yourself that you would like God to help you change? Make a list and, if you are willing, share them with two other persons.

3. In your desire to be a more faithful disciple of Jesus Christ, how will you use what you have learned from your study of this book?

4. Would you be willing to continue to meet with a small group of like-minded persons for further Bible study, discussion, and prayer?

5. Are there others who you think might benefit from these readings and discussions? Would you be willing to lead a group through a similar devotional study?

Endnotes

1. Excerpt from his speech during the Virginia Convention of March, 1775

2. Unanimously adopted and signed by representatives (including Thomas Jefferson, the author) of the 13 original states, July 4, 1776

3. Stanzas 1 and 3 of a poem entitled "Caution on Causes," in *Now, That's a Miracle!*, p. 18, by Richard Stoll Armstrong (CSS Publishing Co., Lima, Ohio, 1996)

4. "Called to Freedom" in *Now That's a Miracle!*, p. 13

5. Armstrong, *The Pastor as Evangelist* (Westminster Press, 1984), p. 56

6. Armstrong, *The Pastor-Evangelist in the Parish* (Westminster/ John Knox Press, 1990), p. 162

7. From my unpublished poem, "Thinking of You"

8. The struggle of that urban congregation was described in my book, *The Oak Lane Story*, published in 1971 by the Division of Evangelism of the Board of National Missions of the former United Presbyterian Church in the U.S.A.

9. Stanzas 1 and 4 of the hymn "O Jesus, I have Promised," by John E. Bode

10. John Milton, *Comus*, line 13

11. *Laodamia*, stanza 15

12. *Love's Labour's Lost*, Act IV, Scene 3, line 344

13. Francis William Bourdillon, *Light*

14. *In Memoriam*, Part XXVII, Stanza 4

15. *Epipsychidion,* line 130

16. Elizabeth Barrett Browning, *Sonnets from the Portugese*, xlviii

17. *Magna Moralia*, Book II, Section 11

18. From his poem, "Invictus"

19. "Secret Service," by Clara Howell

20. See p. 101 and p. 140

21. William Walsham How, 1858

22. *Hamlet, Prince of Denmark*, Act 3, Scene 1

23. "Missing the Moment," from my collection entitled *If I Do Say So Myself* (CSS Publishing Company, 1997), p. 15

24. "Living for Jesus," by T. O. Chisholm, 1917

25. Near the end of Scene III

26. From *Heroes and Hero Worship*

27. The *Faithful Witnesses Mini-Course*, published in 1996 by the Congregational Ministry Division of the Presbyterian Church (USA) is an updated twelve-hour version of the original 16-week *Faithful Witnesses Course* (Geneva Press, 1987)

28. From my collection entitled *Enough, Already!* (Fairway Press, 1993), p. 48

29. "Teach Me to Listen" (Armstrong)

30. Sess. XIV, Can. 6

31. *Institutes of the Christian Religion*, Vol. I, Book III, Chap. IV, Section 7

32. "Secret Sins," from my collection entitled *Songs from Isaiah*

33. *Institutes*, Vol. I, Book III, Chapter IV, Section 12

34. "Secret Sins" (from *Songs from Isaiah*)

35. *Prayer*, by George Arthur Buttrick (Abingdon, 1977)

36. "Knee Exercise," from *Enough, Already!*, p. 74

37. The first line of the gospel song is, "When upon life's living you are tempest tossed."

38. From "What a Friend We Have in Jesus" (Scriven)

39. *Morte d'Arthur*, line 247

40. From Montgomery's *Original Hymns: What Is Prayer?*

41. Walter Mitty was the fantasy-indulging hero in James Thurber's famous story, *The Secret Life of Walter Mitty (1941)*. Danny Kaye played the title role in MGM's frequently rerun technicolor movie version of the same title.

42. William Shakespeare, *Hamlet*, Act 1, Scene 3, lines 78-80

43. From *Now, THAT's a Miracle!*, pp. 28-29

44. *Le Discours de la Méthode*, IV

45. "The Corsair," Canto i, Stanza 8

46. Essay 1, Stanza 45

47. *Heroes and Hero-worship*, Lecture 1

48. See p. 6

49. "It Means What It Means," from *Now, THAT's a Miracle!*, p. 75

50. Matthew Prior, from "Upon a Passage in the Scaligerana"

51. First stanza of a hymn by William H. Foulkes, 1918

52. "Oft in the Stilly Night," from *National Airs*, by Thomas Moore

53. From a hymn by James Montgomery, 1825

54 Edward Fitzgerald, *The Rubaiyat of Omar Khayyam*, lxxi

55. From the hymn "What a Friend We Have in Jesus," by Joseph Scriven

56. From the poem, "As You Forgive," in my to-be-published collection entitled *Is Jesus the One?*

57. Rachel Saint died in 1995, after working for thirty-seven years among the Huaorani. That same year her nephew Steve, Nate's son, and his wife and children moved to Ecuador to work with the Huaorani, helping them to build an airfield and a hospital. Working side by side with him, as Christian friends, are the very men who murdered his father.

58. From the hymn, "Awake, My Soul, Stretch Every Nerve," by Philip Doddridge

59. Alexander Pope, "Essay on Man"

60. From *Christian Behaviour*

61. *The Nature and Destiny of Man*, pp. 186-203

62. Thomas Hood (1799-1845)

63. From the gospel song, "He Lives," by Homer A. Rodeheaver

64. From my yet-to-be-published volume entitled *A Poetic Companion to Paul's Letter to the Romans*

65. Gilbert Keith Chesterton (1874-1936), English journalist and writer

66. *An Essay on Man*, IV. 1

67. "Richard Cory" by Edwin Arlington Robinson

68. *Don Juan*, Canto ii, St. 172

69. "Joyful, Joyful, We Adore Thee," by Henry van Dyke, 1907

70. *Nichomachean Ethics, II. ix*

71. "Temper, Temper!" (Armstrong)

72. From the poem, "Too Quick to Scold" (*If I Do Say So Myself*)

73. "The Toys," by Coventry Patmore

74. "Christian Forbearance," by William Blake

75. "Tam O'Shanter," lines 10,12

76. Richard of Chichester, c. 1197-1253

77. *The Advancement of Learning*, I. v. 8

78. Charlotte Elliott, 1836

79. For a fuller discussion of the nature and role of proof and of faith see my book *Service Evangelism* (Westminster Press, 1979), Chapter 2.

80. From his *Introduction to a Critique of the Hegelian Philosophy of Right* (1844)

81. *The Future of an Illusion*, p. 92

82. From *Prejudices: Third Series*

83. Francis Bacon, who was quoted in Chapter 11, went on to say: "But if we begin with doubts, and are patient with them, we shall end in certainties."

84. Fanny Crosby's hymn "Blessed Assurance, Jesus Is Mine!" was written in 1873.

85. From an unpublished collection of my poems on the *Gospel of John*

86. *The Night Hamburg Died* (Ballantine Publishers), now out of print

87. On Monday, October 18, 1987, the Dow Jones Industrial Average plunged 508 points, or 22.6%, the largest point and percentage loss in the history of the New York Stock Market. More than a trillion dollars was lost by investors.

88. The Great Depression followed the crash of the stock market in 1929. My parents survived it, but some of their relatives and friends were in desperate straits in the early 1930s.

89. I learned this song when I was in college, but I never knew and have not been able to find out who wrote it.

90. From the poem, "The Eternal Goodness," by John Greenleaf Whittier

www.ingramcontent.com/pod-product-compliance
Lightning Source LLC
Chambersburg PA
CBHW051959090426
42741CB00008B/1464